THE INVENTOR OF LOVE

&

OTHER WRITINGS

By Gherasim Luca

Translated by

Julian and Laura Semilian

Introduction by Andrei Codrescu
Essay by Petre Răileanu

BLACK
WIDOW
PRESS

Boston, MA

THE INVENTOR OF LOVE & OTHER WRITINGS by Gherasim Luca, translated by Julian and Laura Semilian, ©2009 Black Widow Press. English language translations ©2009 Julian Semilian and Laura Semilian. "Gherasim Luca: The Flowers of Meat" ©2008 Andrei Codrescu. "Ontopoetics," ©2008 Petre Răileanu. This edition of *L'inventeur de L'amour* et *La Mort Morte* is published by arrangement with Librairie José Corti ©Librairie José Corti, 1994, 2009.

BWP would especially like to thank Bertrand Fillaudeau for his help.

Black Widow Press is an imprint of Commonwealth Books, Inc., Boston, MA. Distributed to the trade by NBN (National Book Network) throughout North America, Canada, and the U.K. All Black Widow Press books are printed on acid-free paper. Black Widow Press and its logo are registered trademarks of Commonwealth Books, Inc.

Joseph S. Phillips and Susan J. Wood, PhD., Publishers
www.blackwidowpress.com

Book Design: Kerrie Kemperman
Front Cover Design: Windhaven Press
Cover photograph of Luca courtesy of Librairie José Corti

ISBN-13: 978-0-9818088-7-1
ISBN-10: 0981808875

Library of Congress Cataloging-in-Publication Data on file

10 9 8 7 6 5 4 3 2 1
Printed in the U.S.A.

THE INVENTOR OF LOVE

&

OTHER WRITINGS

By Gherasim Luca

TABLE OF CONTENTS

GHERASIM LUCA: THE FLOWERS OF MEAT

by Andrei Codrescu

Gherasim Luca was a bull, a *toro*. I met him in New York in the early eighties, where he'd come for some poetic occasion. I find it odd that I can't remember the "official" reason for his visit, which took place in the evening, but whether it was a reading or a conference I can't tell you. All I know is that we had a small entourage of magnetized fans that included, *de rigueur,* two competitive young women with that wonderful academic veneer that slips off like an ill-fitting cape after the second drink, and a few men of whom neither Luca nor I took any notice. Our high spirits proved eventually too much for the company, even for the women, who despite our attempts at promoting universal love, took the cautious taxis home, and we were left alone on a brisk New York spring night, wandering the empty canyons and speaking in sheer bursts of poetry. The *toro* image stands out most clearly in front of the Fifth Avenue entrance to Central Park, when the muscular, bald, small man who must have been well past seventy, lifted his arms into the neon moon and, taking in the entrance to the Plaza Hotel (still a hotel), exclaimed something that Blaise Cendrars, Arthur Cravan, or any number of poets, French or otherwise, did exclaim on that spot at one time or another. The exact words are lost, but no matter, they hover there forever. They were words of delight, of amazement at being alive in New York, very late in the night at the end of the twentieth century, feeling immortal, young, perverse, and above and within all *that*. And more.

Gherasim Luca was an ecstatic, a late surrealist who still thought, in the late 1940s, that surrealism and communism could find common ground by "eroticising the proletariat." That slogan, "éroticiser le prolétariat" was the last hopeful cry of surrealism as a revolution, and Luca uttered it in the full candor of his heart, long after it had become obvious that communism was a bloody tyranny opposed to art and to the inner life of the people it claimed to emancipate. André Breton had lost faith in the revolutionary potential of surrealism during his exile in New York during the war and, while he welcomed such earnest attempts as Luca's (who, like most genuine surrealists after the war, came from central/eastern Europe), he was only paying lip service to what he knew had been a grand failure. Of course, Breton's beliefs did not very much matter by the time he returned to Paris after the war. Surrealism had, from the beginning, worked to free the poetry of the unconscious that boiled within souls such as Gherasim Luca, a poetry inspired in part by the pressure of centuries of anger that had become repressed and compressed in dreams, and in part by the carnivalesque violence of the dadaists led by Tristan Tzara. The swamp of the ghetto pushed forward the flowers of poetry and action embodied by Tzara and Luca, flowers that became wolves, wolves that became loose-cannon-people with hands, and these hands reached for all the available tools, surrealist language and technique being one of them.

Luca's poem, "Lup Vazut Printr-o Lupa," rendered by the Semilians here as "A Periwinkle Perused Through A Periscope," means literally, "a wolf seen through a magnifying glass," a wordplay in Romanian that is untranslatable, hence the Semilians' flower and glass rendition. Writing to me about the Luca translation, Julian signed his message, "Lupul lui Luca," meaning "Luca's Wolf," and in so doing hit, it seems to me, the grave note that the "wolf" possesses but the "periwinkle" doesn't. Luca was a wolf in addition to being a bull, but there was also, to credit the translation, a periwinkle there, which had hardened and gotten teeth in time. The taurean, Picassoesque Luca gesticulating across the road from the Plaza was all meat; his petals, if he was a periwinkle, were fleshed out of thick meat; and his bald head was a battering dome that butted against the moon. His poetry is an outpouring of verbal jewels wrenched from the mines of meat. Had anyone taken him seriously about "eroticising the proletariat," he'd have returned the wolfy mass of industrial workers into the hungry nomads they had been in the neolithic, a prospect that clashed beautifully and hilariously with Lenin and Stalin's talk of ideals and idealized workers. Luca would have de-idealized them, or at least put some meat on the bones of their ideals.

In his poetry, the violence of his psyche liberates each molecule of his body to pursue its own meat-dreams. An average psychoanalyst would rightly be lost in Luca's language, and would stay away from his violation of grammar and good sense. Luca is more than *a case,* he is *the case* against bondage, which is what the brilliant Gilles Deleuze understood instantly in reading him. Meeting Luca in his poetry is a thrilling and harrowing experience, an explosion of intensities that will scare most people away just as we scared our genteel company in New York, but much more gravely, of course. Our company was not really scared of *us,* we were just acting like poets, that is to say, we were still half lambs while being half wolves; they were scared when they remembered Luca's poetry. It was one thing to stay up all night or even go to bed with a potent torro-

poet, and a whole other matter to do so with Gherasim Luca, the author of such lines as: "I kiss the lover's mouth without her discerning whether she was poisoned, chained inside a tower for a thousand years, or whether she fell asleep with her head on the table." That's not why one gets a Ph.D. and starts teaching surrealism at NYU. That's not even why one makes a poetry anthology of surrealism or produces other neat objects that classify and museumify the products of a certain era. Consequently, Luca's poetry is better known among readers of Deleuze, philosophers with a horizon, than among poets, *causeurs* with careers. The Semilians are doing those few American readers who don't read French or Romanian (lazy bums!) a huge favor. They have transferred large chunks of still-bleeding, ripped-apart language (violated syntactically, genderly, and noun-verbed and vice-versa) into a visible thicket of thorny declarations that are right next to Luca's impenetrable forest. That's the most anyone can do in this enterprise of "translation," which is really only a review of the original using words to describe words. *All* translation is that, and if one trusts the reviewer one finds eventually one's way into the forest. The Semilians are stellar reviewers.

The year after Luca visited New York, I was part of the Neustadt Prize Jury at the University of Oklahoma, an international literary prize awarded every year, worth at the time, I believe, sixty thousand dollars. Nicknamed "the little Nobel," the Neustadt was (and may still be) a Nobel weather vane; many of the winners went on to win the Nobel. The jury is international and every juror speaks on behalf of a candidate, attempting to convince the others of their candidate's greatness and need. The other American juror besides myself was Susan Sontag, whose candidate was Nadine Gordimer. The French juror represented René Char, who was ill, and there were other eminences in play, including Milan Kundera. My candidate was the little-known, maybe totally unknown, Gherasim Luca. We deliberated three long winter days while the snow and wind howled outside, and some of us continued at night over wine. Milan Kundera dropped out early because he didn't want to come to Oklahoma to give a speech, one of the conditions of the prize. René Char also lost early, I'm not sure why. My presentation did win me a formidable ally in Susan Sontag, though. She understood quickly, both intellectually and viscerally, the force at work in Luca's poetry. To her credit, this is way before Deleuze uttered a word about Luca. Susan had in her the organ for understanding naturally the angry impulses of the avant-garde and its outlandish metamorphic sexual work. She also had a particular sympathy for Romanians, she'd been an early partisan of E.M. Cioran's work, whose first book in English (translated by Richard Howard) she'd prefaced. With Sontag on my side, it suddenly looked possible that Gherasim Luca could win the Neustadt. He became one of the three top candidates, so we sent him a telegram. Luca lived in a one-room apartment in Paris, without a telephone, on an income of (maybe) $100 a month; he was poor as a mouse. The Neustadt money would have certainly helped, and he met both criteria of genius and need. His response to our telegram was swift: "I don't accept literary prizes." It was a stunner, a gesture that no one, including myself, understood at the time. In retrospect, it makes sense, but out there in the snows of Norman, OK, it looked like the gesture of a madman, something that Susan, in no uncertain terms, attributed to Romanians, "you are all mad," or somesuch. An octogenarian Indian novelist who wrote multi-generational sagas and taught at the University of Texas in El Paso won the prize. Gherasim Luca lived another few years, then committed suicide by throwing his body into the Seine at the same spot that fellow Romanian poets Paul Celan and

Ilarie Voronca had thrown theirs. If you intend to kill yourself and are a Romanian poet of genius, that is the spot, location available on request (and proof of genius).

September 7, 2008, Oz

THE

INVENTOR

OF LOVE

. . . and refusing indignantly any attempt of the external world to isolate him in ivory towers, Non-Oedipus objectifies each of his actions, as if millions of humans are trickling through his enforced solitude.

First Non-Oedipal Manifesto

THE INVENTOR OF LOVE

From one temple to the other, the ebony blood of my virtual suicide drains in virulent silence. As if I had committed an actual suicide, the bullets crisscross my brain day and night, uprooting the ends of my optical nerve, my acoustic, my tactile, these terminals, dispersing inside the skull an odor of detonated gun powder, of clotted blood, of chaos. I haul upon my shoulders this suicide's cranium with a noteworthy sort of grace, and transport from one place to the next a malignant grin, poisoning throughout a radius of numerous kilometers the breath of all beings and things. Perused from the outside I appear to be about to tumble like a man who has been fired upon. It is my customary strut, in which my uncertain silhouette borrows something from the vertigo of those about to be guillotined, of loose rats, of wounded birds. Like a tightrope walker propped up by merely a single umbrella, I fasten myself to my own disequilibrium. I know by rote these routes without knowns, I can wend my way with eyeballs shut. My gesticulating lacks the axiomatic ease of the fish in water, the grace of the vulture or the tiger, it appears wayward, like anything you would glimpse for the first time. I am forced to invent a new mode of ambulation, of breathing, of being, because in the world through which I circulate there is neither water nor earth, neither air nor fire, to warn me beforehand if my means of locomotion should be swimming or flying, or whether I should step forward with both feet. Inventing the fifth element, the sixth, I am forced to revise my compulsions, my customs, my certitudes, because, for instance, to jaywalk from an aquatic life to a terrestrial one without first shifting the determination of your breathing apparatus is equivalent to death.

The fourth dimension (5, 6, 7, 8, 9) the fifth element (6, 7, 8, 9, 10, 11) the third sex (4, 5, 6, 7). I salute my double, my triple. I peruse myself in the mirror and scrutinize my face full of eyeballs, of mouths, of ears, of ciphers. Beneath the moon my body casts a shadow, a half-shadow, a ditch, a quiet lake, an onion. I am indeed indiscernible.

I kiss the mouth of the woman without her discernment as to whether she was poisoned, whether she was chained within a tower for a thousand years, or whether she fell asleep with her head on the table. Everything must be reinvented, nothing exists anymore in the whole world. Not even the things we can do without, that our existence appears to depend upon, they don't exist either. Not even her, the lover, this supreme certitude, her tresses, her blood we scatter with such voluptuousness, our emotive apparatus which her cryptic smirk unleashes every afternoon at 4 o'clock, 4 o'clock, this would be enough, this pre-established and dubious causality of a 4 o'clock, for us to suspect any ulterior embrace, any, but absolutely any human initiative contains this mitigating and mnemonic character of a 4 o'clock, even the fortuitous encounters, the noteworthy romances, even the suddenly striking crises of conscience.

I peruse the filthy blood of the man full of clocks, full of registers, ready-made romances, full of fatal complexes, full of limitations.

With a disgust I have learned to ignore, I propel myself among these pre-staged personalities, among these incessant dependabilities, male and female humans, dogs, schools, mountains, mundane and faded terrors and thrills. For a few thousand years now you put forth this axiomatic man of Oedipus, propagate it like an obscurantist epidemic, the castration-complex man, the man of the natal trauma, upon which you prop up your love affairs, your occupations, your neckties and your purses, your progress, your arts, your churches. I detest this consequent son of Oedipus, I disdain and abjure his pre-established biology. And, if it is thus because man is born, then all that is left for me is to abjure birth, abjure any axiom even if it boasts of the appearance of a certitude. Upholding like a curse this quotidian psychology-consequence of birth, we will never unearth the potential of bursting into the world extrinsic of the natal trauma. The man of Oedipus deserves his destiny.

Because I have not yet torn myself away from the maternal womb and its sublime horizons, I have the appearance of one who is dazzled, somnolent and always somewhere else. That explains why my gestures appear to stutter, my words are endless, my motions too leisurely or too jerky, contradictory, monstrous, adorable. That is why nothing is so disturbing to me when I walk down the street—not even the infamous spectacle of a priest or a statue—as the irritation I feel upon spotting an infant. It is only because I sense that to murder it is no more than a needless and vague act of repetition that I resort to walking quietly on. I prefer to wend my way among humans like a danger in state of suspension rather than as an actual murderer, like the precipitator of an endless agony.

From this non-Oedipal position of existence that I occupy, I stalk with a black and malefic eye, I listen with an un-acoustic ear, I touch, with an insensible, invented, artificial hand, the thigh of this woman, and do not retain the perfume, the velvet—these fixed attractions of her magnificent flesh—but the electric spark, the falling stars of flesh, glimmering off and on, but only once in the course of the entire eternity, the fluid and the magnetism of this thigh, its cosmic radiations, the light and the dark inside it, the rivulets of blood that traverse it, its unique position in space and time, that are revealed to me under this monstrous magnifying glass which is my brain, my heart, my inhuman breath. I do not comprehend the allure of existence beyond these unique revelations pertaining to each instant. If the woman who entrances us doesn't invent herself before our eyes, if our eyes do not abandon the timeworn cliché of the image upon the retina, if they do not allow themselves to be magnified, astonished, surprised, and drawn into a region perpetually virgin, then all life appears to me as an arbitrary fixation upon some age of our childhood or of humanity, a mimicking of the lives of others. Indeed, then life becomes a theatrical routine in which we act out the roles of Romeo, Cain, Caesar, and other macabre personages. With these corpses we cross like coffins the distance that separates birth from death, and it doesn't surprise me that the servile brain of humans could conceive a picture of life after death, this simulacrum, this prefabrication, this repulsive posturing of the pre-established and counter-revolutionary.

I breathe in the scent of my lover's tresses as if we flared up into the world for the first time. Anything can occur in this world without a past, without points of reference, without knowns. To breathe in the scent of the lover's tresses with forethought, incognizant and contemptible, then to kiss her on the mouth, to drift from the preliminaries to possession, from possession to exhaustion, and then to a new state of arousal seems to me the very prescription for the straitjacketing technique of this congenital cliché which is the human existence. If in executing this simple act, of breathing in the scent of the lover's tresses, we do not gamble life itself, we do not engage the destiny of the last atom of our blood and of the most distant star, if in this modicum of a second in which we execute in their totality our doubts, our riddles, our disquiet, our most contradictory aspirations, then indeed love is, as the swine advertise it, no more than a digestive function to perpetuate the species. For me the lover's eyes are as somber, as foggy, as vast as any star, and only in light-years should you measure the radium of the glances she tosses me. It seems to me almost as if only the relationship of causality connecting the tides to the moon phases is more curious than this exchange of glances (of fulgurations) in which, as in a cosmic bath, my destiny and the universe resolve to collide as if in tryst. Brushing with the tip of my finger the lover's nipple, what occurs then on the strata of stimulation is an actuality, but a partial actuality, because anything could occur then—this gesture will not simulate except on the level of the pictorial, the descriptive, the gestures of other humans as well as my own—brushing then my lover's nipple I would be stunned if it weren't suddenly midnight, if her flesh weren't suddenly layered with lilies, or if the bellman didn't bring me a letter enclosed in a thousand envelopes. On these uncharted territories which the lover, the chair, the drapes, the mirrors present us with, I blissfully abolish the eye that witnessed, the lips that kissed, the brain that reasoned, like matchsticks that serve me, but only a single time.

Everything must be invented. The fact that the lover's body is covered with scars: only Oedipal thinking can present this in a sadomasochistic context, only thinking already thought can content itself with a label, with a statistic. I like certain kinds of wide knife blades upon which the manufacturer's emblem appears like a humorous vestige of old medieval inscriptions. I like to trace this knife along my lover's skin during sultry afternoons, when I appear to be most tranquil, inoffensive, tender. Her body flinches lightly, exactly like the times when she receives me between her lips, as though inside a tear. I am so attuned to her sudden twitch, so moved by her hidden torment, which I suspect is atrocious, so good! As if hanging my hands in the water during the course of a boat ride, her skin opens to one side of the knife and the other, allowing the passage through flesh of this oneiric blood-ride, this exquisite blood-boat I kiss with an open mouth.

From a distance I contemplate the satiated brain of man denouncing me to psychology as if I were some sort of vampire. During other afternoons, I contemplate his pharmaceutical brain, from a distance, while my ardor drifts like a flame inside its own darkness, hounded by its own disquiet, setting slender, vertiginous traps for itself, simultaneous questions and answers, long corridors where I unbind my hair, stairways spiraling to endlessness, mortared-up chambers where I commit suicide innumerable times, an undomesticated vegetation, a river, from a distance I contemplate his reductive circumvolutions, cynical and vain, cataloguing me as yet another Narcissus, another fetishist, scatophiliac, necrophiliac, somnambulist or sadist, yet another sadist.

With secret and unequaled pleasure, which reminds me only of the existential travesty of the conspirator and the magician, I take the liberty to torture my lover, to bloody her flesh and to kill her without being sadistic. I am sadistic only to the extent that you might say: he killed her because he had a knife with him. I am possessed by a sadistic psychology that surprises me at times when brutalizing a woman, but this act necessitating the participation of my entire being does not in turn necessitate the participation of my being's conclusions. There is no act that claims the last word, but in each act, even the most elementary, I risk my life. I like this quiet summer evening, looking out of the window at the firmament. While my eyes allow themselves to be captivated by a single star, my hands, thin, beguiling, feverish, the true hands of a murderer, peel an apple as if skinning a woman. With my sex erect, cold sweat pouring all over my body, breathing ever faster and faster, I bite into the apple while engaged in contemplating the distant star with the sort of candor worthy only of a demon. I have no idea why I am thinking now of the two notorious sadists of vegetation: William Tell and Newton, but if the law of gravity can be inferred from Newton's legendary apple and the acceleration of velocity from William Tell's arrow, my entrancement may be catalogued as sadism, the same as any other form of reductionism integral to the mythical and the legendary.

I love this invented lover, this paradisiacal projection of my infernal brain, which I use as nourishment for my demon. Upon her angelic flesh I endlessly project my convulsions, my poisons, my fury, but particularly my unceasing, terrible passion for sacrilege. This passion without limits for sacrilege suckles inside me at the temperature of negation, and of negation's negation, all of the unbound hatred for everything absolutely that exists, because everything that exists contains in its subterranean implications a grave that we must defile, and because we ourselves, at this very instant, have the cadaver's tendency to accept ourselves, to see ourselves as axioms.

I love this woman who prepares for me each morning, out of her own precious veins, a warm bath of blood. After this elementary morning-toilet of the demon, I do not even recognize my own blood.

In order for love to shed the paralyzing temper of the traumatic mother and of her menacing, castrating accomplice, the father, the lover that my hidden-explosive being, my crystallized being, my being devoured by inexhaustible thirst for love, can only be an unborn woman.

I am not speaking about a woman who has not yet been born, about one of those perfumed tumors of the idealist philosophy that everyone wears in the center of their hearts like a nostalgic wound; this ideal woman, fixed and remote, whom the romantics in their lyrical opium dens conjured for us as almost accessible and for whom you always search in vain all across this earth, in vain do you search for this absolute woman whose reason for being is by definition that you should never encounter her, because if you were to encounter Gradiva or Cinderella, she would cease being equal to her own perfume, she would be nothing other than a model wife, a model mother, in the same way that the most apparently insignificant error in theory is a victory for death; this ideal woman towards whom men only aspire to in order never to find, or in finding her, to lose her again in order to sustain the religious idea, so deplorably human, that love is a well of sorrow and vain illusion; this eternal woman of dreams who, instead of reconciling them, digs even deeper the chasm between day and night, eternalizing, it seems, even more shamefully, the duality and agonizing struggle of man within the wall of his own prison.

The unborn woman of my heart has nothing in common with this romantic absolute of idealist philosophy, except for the mantle of stars that both of us will toss over the lover's adored shoulders; beyond this mantle of stars that ventilates her flesh with its spicy aromas, my unborn lover does not detach herself from humanity's putrid heart, and when I say humanity's putrid heart I am not referring to man's inutile and barren life, but to his most elevating dreams, his secret dreams. The existence of the banker and the poet in the bosom of contemporary society has not been, for a long time now, a contradiction, and the idea of siding with the poet appears to me all the more dismal. In this tyrannical world dominated by the simultaneous antinomies that I provoke in my surroundings, even the most scintillating poet is a purulent excrescence no different than the banker's erotomania, man's night life and day life, his dreams and his vigils being irreconcilable, because being already reconciled in this eternal promiscuity in which the tiny eternal desires, the dear eternal subversive ideas, the modest incestuous dreams, eternal immoral dreams, mingle and mix with the idiotic and impudent obstacles of the external world, ludicrously eternalized and whose function is to conciliate this suffocated life, fruitlessly wasted, and the dream of minimal requirements that defrauds it and upon which the Oedipal man props himself up in the most permanent mode, this horrific vicious circle projected across the purview of the entire existence.

This unborn woman, which only my unbounded fury against the eternal immobility of humans disentangles from the great universal movement in which I integrate my being, escapes this limiting and suffocating vicious circle which the constrained biology of humans sets as a perfidious trap, this biology which still fluctuates between the normal and the abnormal and whose dialectic solution (partially achieved) will change nothing of the precariousness of existence. Because I reject the precariousness of existence in all of its aspects, I see the liberation of man inexorably connected to the simultaneity of all solutions, and please don't tell me that the social revolution must be accomplished first and only then the moral one, etc., that these leaps of man inside his own destiny must resolve for him all at once the demands of the moment, because a married proletarian, or a proletarian who admires his father, off to accomplish a revolution, will carry within his own plasma the anaesthetizing microbe of the family, and such a revolution is fated to failure, either because the class enemy ends up being manifestly victorious, or because he is powerful enough within the flaccid blood of the proletarian himself to gain the apparent victory. This simultaneous correspondence of the most disparate revolutionary aspirations, in which we must make room for the most diverse, such as the manner in which we comb our hair, kiss one another, gaze at each other (because no one could convince me that after you accomplish your first assassination you can gaze the same way into the eyes of the woman crossing the street), in this maniacal precaution not to leave any desire in a state of suspension, to realize ourselves entirely in every moment, to become progressively more intransigent, more excruciating, more irreconcilable, contains in itself the guarantee that what we have gained will never again be taken away from us. Putting aside the precariousness of man's existence, his rudimentary biology leaning towards the reactionary, the funereal, with the vague and progress-inducing hope that everything will be solved tomorrow, when I know that this very tomorrow will always be late in arriving, because any tendency to surpass and shatter our own limits is prohibited because of our good sense, because of our modesty and rationalism. It is only because I have dared to shatter these oppressive limits that oppose the integral liberation of man, now when my fellow beings commit suicide in the most execrable manner for the sake of abstract ideas such as beauty, justice, honor, while in the shadows their rulers split the profits, I awaken so solitary, solitary amidst a vast graveyard, without knowing whether, if I touched these fresh cadavers, my hand will produce a miraculous solution or merely the lascivious quiver of the necrophiliac, but with the hope, with the irrational certitude that my appearance in the world contains in its hidden fibers, in its multiple determinants—among which the astral are the most favorable—the dissolution of this world and that this solitary wanderer who walks a furious and profanatory melancholy along the silent alleys of the cemetery is nothing other than an enamored lover.

A monstrous enamored lover enamored of a monstrous enamored lover, unnatural, inhuman, unborn, of this lover who is a stranger to the natal cemetery, this source of all of love's clichés, all the fixed gestures whose refined but modest diversity is not capable of maintaining the hopes you place in the future of this funereal species, because only birth can explain, can support, can make necessary its replica—death, because it is only because of birth that humans prepare a place for themselves in the cemetery, and the funeral stone that they permanently lug inside their chests prescribes the limited number of their movements, under this funeral stone we have become accustomed to lugging about like a necessity that suffocates the captive lung of humans, repeats itself, this fatal paralytic will love in a fatal manner in everything the one woman, the same one the whole world loves, mama, in the same manner that, locked for life in a tower with a woman, any woman, you will love her fatally, in the same fatal manner that the arts and human ugliness flower, in the same fatal manner that humans get married, live in concubinage and execute the few hundred sensual and sentimental motions that define their limits, and even the so-called *psychopathia sexualis* that introduces into this ankylozed world some sort of variation, even that comforting negation which is sexual madness and vice, seems to me insufficient (though it is the only thing that allows me to gaze in the face of humans with a certain kind of indulgence), all these few hundreds of tics that cause humans to look alike, like two drops of sweat look alike, contain the embryos of their decomposition in the mother's image, in the maternal causality and the insignificant complications engendered by the other sinister personage which is the father, do nothing but turn this condemned species into a monotone and ugly landscape, and I will never cease being stunned at how it is possible that humans can bear this galley-slave destiny, and how it is possible that the number of the hopeless, of the suicides and the assassins is so small.

Enamored of this lover only after I have refused the axiomatic condition of existence, denouncing the authors of my time in the same manner that I have murdered my Creator, I permit myself the freedom of not loving an image already made by the Creator and of witnessing the appearance in the world of this lover in the same way that I would witness in astonishment the disengagement of a distant planet from chaos, of participating in the attraction and repulsion played out between the different parts of her ever-surprising anatomy, in the dissipating, the crystallizing, the simultaneous burning and cooling of this adored nebula, which is my lover in a perennial state of becoming, in a sublime negation of her entire being, perennially invented, waking up each morning with a new image of being enraptured, because inside this perennially invented lover you can find all those live fragments found in the biological ruins of long-vanished humanity, fragments of bodies, of aspirations, of love's fossils, but not a complete female body where her little virtues doubled by her little vices are locked in one single place in desolate promiscuity, the warm and the cold, her sorrows and exaltations, her tears and joys. These female bodies that rendezvous inside my lover leave at the door, like a useless corpse, all their knowns, the ideas they had formulated about love, everything they knew beforehand they would find in my room, following with bated breath, with the perplexity provoked by a mirror that reflects back to you an unequalled, coruscating stranger in whom you do not fail to recognize yourself only to fail to recognize yourself a moment later, following the layer of blood at the core of their being, dusty after so many centuries of waiting, wrapped in the thick blanket of ancestral mildew, fatal custom of longing nostalgically for the maternal womb, when this maternal womb cannot be accessible in its quotidian, current, total actuality. These female bodies, these fragments, diamonds, mouths, eyelashes, coiffures and veils, losing in part their inutile individuality, renouncing, that is, the ancient, nefarious formula of the lover who wants to be loved as she is, even though what is to be loved in her distances her from her own being, regains in exchange the freedom to emerge out of the baneful limits of man's initial complex that causes her to search in me for that same lugubrious personage of a thousand masks which is the father. These female bodies dynamited by me, fragmented and mutilated by my monstrous thirst for a monstrous love, have finally found the freedom to search for and find the marvelous at the core of their being and nothing could make me believe that love can be anything other than this mortal passageway to the marvelous, in its lascivious perilousness, in its chaotic, aphrodisiac catacombs, where the never-before-encountered and the never-before-seen are the current characters of a continual surprise, this passageway to life and death in the marvelous being for me the neural center of existence, the frontier point where life begins to be worth living, because this frontier point of existence contains in its secret warnings the transcending of human existence in all its oppressive aspects, the solution to the great Oedipal drama that unravels the human being, that suffocates the human being, that walls the human being alive in its own grave.

The five women, who visit my voluptuously amorous despair under the most unexpected, the most singular and absurd circumstances, render maneuverable this tentacular and radiant lover who bathes my existence in perfume. During the hours of the day and the night, while my fellow beings crawl with titanic efforts towards their initial condition which they could never reach, while on the surface of the earth these fellow beings mimic with stereotypical, sublimated gestures, with direct, sensual, sentimental, cultural, belligerent, religious gestures the initial scene whose incendiary pleasure left a blister that will never heal upon their memory, while these fellow beings pay with their own blood for the consequences of their incomplete amnesia, in my dialectical reality the initial kinship of water and fire reestablishes itself of its own will, as does the kinship of flesh and ectoplasm, of life and death, of love. During the hours of the day and the night, as if attracted by a phallic divinity in which they rendezvous in order never to separate again, love and magic, unknown women appear in my life, unrecognizable even to themselves, with a mask of black velvet over their faces. They perform the ritual of love with gestures that are reminiscent of anything, even of a death sentence and a fainting spell on the bottom of the sea or the burning of a precious papyrus, but never of that elemental exercise that man performs with the same easy indifference in whorehouses, in churches, or in his degrading dramas of passion. Like amorous mythical personages of a species that invents itself before my own eyes, these women perform gestures whose immediate or ulterior significance escapes them momentarily but whose demoniacal resonance fills them with voluptuousness. These women sign a blood pact with me. They extract the blood they sign with at random from dreams, from thighs, from fingers, from under the temples. Only after I have extracted from them those few drops of blood through which they give themselves to me as to a demon, only after they cease belonging to themselves, will these women begin to find themselves again, to be enraptured and bewitched by their own internal murmur. They near their own destinies, their shadows and flesh, and completing one another, they seem to emanate light under their torn mantles, and it is only then that they experience the exalting sentiment that they are unique, that they are chosen, irreplaceable, which could never occur to them in the amorous exercises in which a man mounts a woman in order for both of them to reflect their nothingness upon each other. These women who have broken free, whom appearances, streets, customs attempt to denounce at every turn as if they were the village madwomen, project unceasingly upon the screen of my heart that stunning lover, invented and inventable, to whom I join my life.

And I find that the end of this phrase, where I confess to my lover eternal fidelity, has a unique fragrance now as I pronounce it, because I see here the alarmed figures of my fellow beings who have been vainly attempting during the last few years to cast my effigy between the cadavers of their customary triviality, between their familiar clichés, which are Don Juan and Casanova, disillusioned by the devotional gazes that I use to caress with limitless adoration a woman whom I never seem to have known for long, baffled by this replica of the romantic, innocent and puerile, by my satanic fidelity, and I am convinced that it would be far more comforting to the customary course of human turpitude if I were a ferocious assassin or an absurd arsonist, as long as I were reducible to one of their pre-established knowns, but they will never forgive me the shifting sands of my supple gestures, atrocious and vertiginous like volcanoes, the gliding along terrains from one dynamited encounter to the next, this quivering tangle of fragmentary women, unknown or partially known and who are attracted to me by an irresistible force, in circumstances without any equivalence in the ready-made world of current or exceptional phenomena, but which remind at times of the processes of displacement and condensation suffered by phenomena in one's oneiric life, a dress, a thin veil, a green eye and a blue eye, a perfume or a leisurely poison, a fainting spell, a wound on the thigh, disheveled coiffures—so many vague and distant allusions, so many favorable currents that draw to the surface this head of mysteries, my lover's head draped in nebulae, my adored lover's head, the head of my tentacular, unborn lover, whose supreme evidence is the immense umbilical cord through which I suck out her heart.

I ROAM THE IMPOSSIBLE

Illustrated with five non-Oedipal objects

The attraction exerted upon me by the object in all of its symptomatically dialecticized aspects and the few personal determinants about which it is useless to speak of again, because I have already spoken about it with sufficient insistence somewhere else (*The Passive Vampire,* manuscript, 1941), brought me, a few years ago, to the discovery of a new object of knowledge that I had named Objectively Offered Object (O. O. O.), whose purpose was to inaugurate among human beings a series of relationships supported by an active collective unconscious in an alert state, relationships which by means of the most elementary effort of interpretation will divulge to us the precious essences of life, the fluid that draws us closer to and further from our destinies. These researches, endeavored around the object, have been continued somewhat later under entirely different and subjective circumstances, with the succinct presentation of the observations which I have extracted (*To Oneiricize the World,* manuscript, 1943), anyone can realize, especially if he resorts to his own personal systematized experience, that the objective offering of an object introduces into the relationships between human beings that chaotic and misleading complicity interlacing the members of a secret society, the secret in this case being all the more terrible as it is confused with the millennial mystery of man itself.

The reference to the two above-quoted works is only partial; it is more a reference to the spirit of those works rather than to the letter, because in the second I do no more than transcribe, and that only in brief manner, a minimal portion of the mystery that disquieted my life by means of the object, while in the first, in which the object objectively offered is presented with a certain theoretical and interpretative amplitude, I am too restrained by psychology's fixed data, too inebriated by psychology's real or fatally provisional results, and despite all delirious, paranoiac and visionary liberties that I possess at times, the objective world continues to refuse itself and to reject us on account of the purely Oedipal character of our researches. Because to attempt to accommodate these efforts to the present stage of my research would be mundane, didactic and moral, meaning it would also be necessarily inexact. They adapt of themselves through the radiations that the duration's dialectic transmits towards me and it is enough for me to think that one of these efforts reproduces the first object objectively offered to the infernal forces, a pact I signed with Satan, in order for me to understand that demonic dialectic to which my thought process is so faithfully fixed, and, from the non-Oedipal position of knowledge in which I find myself, my researches around the object, although Oedipal, can only now be captured in truth in what they have in them that is most brilliant, most precious, most filled with consequences.

As a means of verifying these supple leaps that our defunct conclusions execute in time, the five objects I received during the last few days from a woman appear in my room not only to topple the object discovered by me in 1941 in an Oedipal condition of existence, but also to affirm for the first time its virulence, its certitude and all its possibilities of surpassing this condition. It is certain that the sexual symbolism as well as the entire latent Oedipal content of the object persists in the offering of these objects, except that here the manifest content refuses to allow itself to be exhausted by a translation which is reducible to two or three initial complexes, in order for the discovery of these complexes to become truly revelatory to our erotic life, it must first be retained and then negated in dialectic mode, a revolutionary mode of thinking, always rejecting with indignation any attempt at being imprisoned inside a certitude, no matter how fascinating it may be. Because I will never stop confusing the sense of life with the sense of love, the definitive superimposition of the love of Oedipus causes me to desperately negate the unbearable character of the absolute it contains, the most direct consequence of my fierce negation, of this imperious negation of the negation, is that it is revealed to me as if I were gazing at a crystal ball on my lover's cheek, the radiant sense of love which, without ignoring Oedipus, rejects his disappointing tendency of jeopardizing our destiny, without ignoring Oedipus and stepping over his corpse which we continue to contain, it is revealed to us on the screen of this crystal ball the dimension of love, a manifest content of love whose latent translation cannot be reduced to the two or three initial complexes which for me are confused with the macabre image of don't-stretch-beyond-your-bed-mattress or whatever-you-do-you-will-still-die, this new latent translation with a pronounced occult character, finding sexual, materialist and dialectic equivalencies without being forced to deal with the father's promiscuity, nor the mother's, nor the older brother's, to which the attempt is made to connect our existence instead of being shown how to betray them, without having to ask permission of the family, represented so perfectly by the classic methods of dream interpretation, of neuroses, of the gestures with hundreds of thousands of corridors though which we reveal ourselves.

If I suffered from the necessity of producing a systematic interpretation of these objects, I would never take the direction of any of the classical methods of exploring the unconscious, whose reducibility to Oedipus I would, in the best case scenario, presuppose, and would be much more tempted to resort to the somnambulistic method of Objectanalysis as I defined and utilized it in *Two Invisible Women Knock on My Door, a Dying Woman Offers Them an Envelope on my Behalf* (manuscript, 1944). But my lyrical-subjective and amorous-objective position before the five received objects necessarily prevents me from systematizing the voluptuous vertigo I experience in merely contemplating them and what necessarily is being suggested to me is to maintain and aggravate my vertigo to the fainting point, to allow myself to be passionately drawn towards all the lascivious and chaotic traps which are being set for me. Indeed, my room, where during the last few months the most inaccessible secrets of love are being unveiled, this room where I feel at all times as a traveler, as a guest, a guest to a permanent dialogue with Satan and his faithful demons, offers me as usual the disconcerting and irritating view (the fire and pitch of popular imagination) that makes possible the conspiratorial rendezvous of the infernal forces between the walls of my room. The five disconcerting and irritating objects that do nothing but continue the messages, the gazes, the doorbells, the shadows and absolutely everything else that traffics through my room with the single mission of maintaining in a disconcerting and irritating atmosphere, so favorable to my satanic activities, the five objects are nothing but the inanimate projection upon the walls of my room of the five women satanized by me, and how secretly and voluptuously I savor my initiate smile, following with my gaze the disappearance, as if from beneath a curtain of smoke, of all the blood upon my lover's cheek at the moment when, offering to me the first object, she observes in a state of total stupefaction how every element on the object's body belongs—even she doesn't know how it is possible—to one of the five women maintaining my demon.

This medium-lover, whose extreme amorous passivity causes her to be more receptive than my own thought processes, whose somnambulistic and devoted love causes her to perceive, in advance of my own thought processes, the messages addressed to me from the depths of my being, this lover who anticipates me, who thinks me, who communicates to me only the day after I had radiated from afar a series of actions which she executes in a state of ambulatory automatism and irresistible frenzy, but the desire that spurred the unfurling of those actions I only discover when she reveals it to me, only then do I discover how personal, how much my own that desire is and that all attempts of engaging her by means of a sadomasochistic rapport in activating this desire is an error. The insertion of the lover within a sado-masochistic context may explain (in part) the affective terrain of which I make use, but the actions themselves escape these explanations because they bear my own emblem and not that of the one who executes them. In each of these message-actions I recognize unto the smallest details my own personal method of taking action as opposed to hers which is nearly the reverse, so that to find the next day that without my knowledge I had a desire which I sent mediumistically to my lover has become for the certitude and the objective consequence of an objective amorous rapture which is impossible for me not to compare with the results obtained through any other objective method which arouses the visionary, active and real functioning of thought.

Absorbed in life-and-death engagement in the labyrinths of my thought processes, my lover-medium allows herself to be frantically consumed by the flames of the magic circle within which the nefarious acts of my thought processes unfold of late, the five objects she sent me being absolutely ungraspable if not perused from within the circumference of this circle, from within the circumference of these acts and these thoughts, the sexually symbolic character visible from the outside being incapable of explaining my fetishistic swoon, the qualitative leap and the limitless excitement to which I am taken by their simple contemplation. These aphrodisiacal objects received from my preferred medium being for me the expression of my own aphrodisiacal thought process, the expression of my activities and thought processes from a permanent position of being inciter and incited, inspirer and inspired, provocateur and provoked by rapture. I have, in support of all these affirmations, a thousand examples to sustain my integral presence inside her mediumistic automatism, the most recent being the fleeting passage, possibly even erroneous, through my life of a certain person, a person who, in a few days, in the presence of these aphrodisiacal objects (which are nothing but the projection of my own aphrodisiacal tendencies dispatched from afar to my medium who dispatches them back in material form) will negate the error of the first encounter and allow herself to be drawn to me in an amorous encounter that surpasses all her expectations, one in which she throws all caution to the winds but which engages her destiny for the rest of time. It is only by perusing the five objects as a mediumistic materialization of my most intimate, my most secret tendencies, that the attraction, subtle and definitive, that this visitor feels towards me becomes intelligible. I say intelligible, not resolved, because the very presence of these objects on the map of my amorous encounters makes no difference except as a supra-determinant (-although irradiant) factor, of the occult nature of any determinant-partial-irradiant symptomatic act, like the darkness, the mask, the veil, whether she will walk in barefoot or keep on her stockings and shoes, her dress, the choice (unconsciously astrological) of the hour, the number of knocks on the door, etc. It is only that the manifest affective resonance that this partial determinant occupies in my heart transforms the five objects into an auspicious principle of this amorous encounter, as though their concrete manifestation on my walls were a chemical aphrodisiac with the added delirious properties of a narcotic potion.

The five objects scatter inebriating substances throughout the room, velvets and voluptuous pillows, perfumes and shadows impalpable to the senses but registered by the heart, which beats faster, with all-pervading amnesia regarding our previous life, with the passion with which we throw ourselves into each other's arms while reinventing our embraces, and because the five objects are the most secret expression of my thought processes, they evade, just like my thought processes, a sensorial translation in their brute form, preserving only that of presentiment, of evasion, I would go so far as to say of systematic evasion, without my claim being suspected of some sort of treason of physical matter—my claim of according the thought-process a superior status to the rudimentary recording devices which are their senses and their theoretical equivalents. I make believe that these objects contain an aphrodisiac which is addressed not to the senses but to those parts of my thought processes that created them from afar, those parts which only because of the lack of a synthesized expression do I call the unconscious, those parts that set in motion the body and the spirit, my own and my lover's body and spirit, aphrodicized by that aphrodisiac of thought processes, I make believe they perform within the interior of an aphrodicized chamber not an inebriation of the senses and of the sentiments, not a libertine nor platonic desperation, these backward forms, illusory and dualistic, of rapturous amorous encounters being implied but not sought, what the amorous seek being only an amorous encounter equal to their own mystery and if, roaming along the black arteries of their hidden being, they encounter on their path the affective or libertine effusions under their known aspects, they utilize them as some diurnal remnants of a dream engaged in the real trauma, the full-of-mystery trauma of desire, desire being possible only if we incite in our midst, regardless of what artificial means are used, simulated or not, an evasive atmosphere, inebriating and aphrodisiacal, the only one capable of bringing us close to the evasive, inebriating and aphrodisiacal content of love.

In this demoniacal atmosphere in which amorous rapture reinvents itself for me out of its own existence and life consumes itself in me as if each time is the first time they encounter me, objects as well as events, gestures, silhouettes take on the actual proportions that desire destines for them with so much amplitude, the simplest elements being decomposable beyond the proton, neither from the analytical point of view belonging to a laboratory of the spirit, nor from the scientific necessity of knowing, so detestably disengaged, but only because this panic-placement before the simplest elements maintains my repulsion towards everything of that ilk, towards everything that prevents the thought process from advancing towards its own becoming. To gaze at the object and everything that surrounds me as if our pupils were filled with dynamite, to gaze in order to destroy and become bewildered, in order to become unhinged, in order to become systematically intoxicated and insane, brings us closer to the mystery of the inner and outer world, this permanent complicity with the destructive forces of evil being the most certain guaranty of my objectivity. To let myself become bewildered by objects is for me to close upon their intimate sense from which is suspended the intimate sense of my own being, much more certain than the exacting and exterior attempt of subjecting atoms or symbols to the laboratory experience. Entirely bewildered by these five objects, inflamed to the point of erection, irritated and chimerical at the sight of them, these objects perpetuate in me a state of visionary receptivity which incites me to grasp the distant messages contained in them and the consequence of making contact with these objects is that the very core of my quotidian life is engaged and not just its sublimated aspects.

I would make love with these five objects of love, I would set on fire these flames, I would take them on a rowboat junket, I would smell them and paint my hair and arms green. In truth it is necessary, after contemplating them, to make an enormous effort of imagination in order not to murder this woman. To murder the author of the five objects seems to me the supreme homage I could bestow upon her, impaling her thorax of black marble with a knife in order to snatch her heart in my teeth for the rest of her life.

To love.

THE DEAD DEATH

Five non-Oedipal suicide attempts

I pursue, with a mental voluptuousness filled with delights, in an uninterrupted state of affective and physical arousal, the leaps that I perform within and without myself as if towards a unique solution. All these contemplative leaps, active and lubricious, which I perform simultaneously while in a state of vigil and slumber, even my evasive or ignoble or profoundly aphrodisiacal or completely unintelligible mode of saluting my fellow beings and my shadow from afar, of touching and displacing, with an affected indifference, a fork, a machine gun or a woman's hair, all these convulsive leaps which I provoke inside my own being integrated convulsively in the grandiose universal convulsion and whose dominant dialectic is perpetually accessible to me, though I might discern nothing except accords disguised in darkness, have begun of late to present me with all of their prohibited regions, their chaotic and impenetrable regions, as if, in perusing the narcissistic surface of a mirror, you are tempted to pursue yourself even in its heterosexual negations, you would, out of ignorance, chew the surface silver layer and contemplate with stupefaction your disappearance.

We're not speaking here about a kind of ignorance on the plane of knowledge, of man's religious maneuver of confessing with self-importance his lack of knowledge. I have no knowledge of any intellectual curiosity within myself and proclaim without any scruples my complete indifference towards all the grandiose questions that my fellow beings ask themselves mechanically in regard to a few fundamental problems. I could die a few hundred times without bothering to confront some fundamental problem like death, in its philosophical dimensions, because this mode of becoming disturbed with disquietude over the all-encompassing mystery always appeared to me external to the real dialectic solutions and profoundly impregnated with spiritism, because of the methodological idealism it contains, regardless of whether the method of research claims to be materialistic or not.

Death as obstacle, as oppression, as tyranny, as limit, as universal anxiety and my real enemy, my quotidian, insupportable, inadmissible, unintelligible enemy, I am saying that in order for death to become truly vulnerable and thus open to untangling, it must be positioned, as far as I can see, in the scrupulous and grandiose dialectical interactions which I continuously maintain with it, in the same way that I in fact maintain interactions with any external factor, favorable or not, regardless of the position it occupies in the ridiculous hierarchy of values. An umbrella found on the street seems to me, in its relationship to death, at least as grave as the somber diagnosis of a medical doctor. In my genuine interactions with death (with its costume, violence, destiny, universal causality, palpitation, flowers) the fortuitous pronunciation of the noun *the moribund* in place of the noun *the lover* is enough to unnerve my mediumistic skills, and the danger of death that threatens my lover and that I ascertain through a slip of symptomatically subjective premonition (I desire her death) and a symptomatically objective one (her death actually occurs) inspires me to resort to a symptomatically subjective magic counterattack (I don't desire her death—internal ambivalence, culpability) and an objective one as well (the external causality is neutralized, external ambivalence, fortuitous chance), through the crafting of a simulacra-talisman, through an automatic procedure of self-invented magic, which I took the time to describe in *The Magnetic Eye,* (manuscript, 1943) so I won't bother with it now, the crafting of this talisman, integrated with the other forceful monotheistic supra-determinants, anxiety-producing, aging, accidental, necessary, mechanical and erotic, these elements that together stand council for how to comport oneself before death (and its possible court), being the only objective expression of the dialectic contact with death, the only one to solemnly take on the problem of death in regards to discovering its source, its very spring.

This state of panic-desolation and of moral catalepsy to which the current impenetrability of my own dialectical leaps takes me has nothing to do with an intellectual deportment before the problem of knowledge. The fact that the last thirty days of my life have been wrapped in even more mystery than my previous days, might have, in different circumstances, disturbed me like a drug, like a new derangement. As a matter of fact I maintain about me in a systematic mode an atmosphere of incessant fog, of perplexing paradoxes, of intentionally puerile and simulated mysteries, insoluble and voluptuously evasive. On a theoretical plane, the mystery is for me no longer a source that can be exhausted through analysis, analysis like any other rational or irrational method of interpretation being nothing but partial possibilities of embodying the mystery, possibilities whose usefulness I discern especially in the sense that each truth discovered by us embodies the mystery only in order to irradiate it in the incipient negation, giving it a special theoretical attraction which makes it resemble those irresistible and hysterical women at the turn of the century over which amorous rapture pasted multiple layers of lace, of silk, of perfume, of vertigo.

That's why I declare that it is not the interpretative failure of the last thirty days that causes my despair (in relation to the last thirty days I possess a vast rational and irrational analytical material whose usefulness does nothing but to satisfy my conceit but not my anguish) which incites me to despair, perplexity, the chaos of my thinking process and a ceaseless physical oppression within my chest, as if someone were taking bites from it, it is the failure of my notorious appearance on this globe in such dazzling circumstances at the start of this year, under the threat of dispersal in most lamentable mode during the last thirty days, it is the fabulous, monstrous deception incited by my own personage, inebriated by the idea that he is voyaging with untold agility the border between slumber and watchfulness, between yes and no, between possible and impossible, to find himself face to face with the very opposite effect, inside a world of empty illusions, of subjective games and unforgiving fundamental errors that transmute my matchless and unimaginable existence into a wound. In this parallel world full of illusions into which I feel I have been thrown, without knowing the particular objective error committed (not even on the subjective level of culpability), without knowing what happened to me, and especially why, I feel nothing except the catastrophic effects of this error in the avalanche of aggressions and cruelties, probably necessary, that the external world unleashes against me. Without exception all the personages who surround me betray me. All objects, all women and friends, the weather, the cats, the landscape, the squalor, absolutely everything that stalks me with amorous craving or disdain takes advantage of my immense weakness (consequence of a theoretical error which presently escapes me) and hammers me with simultaneous violence and repulsive cowardice, this last probably all the more necessary. All of a sudden I find myself in a frozen room, famished, alone, filthy, the virtuality of my Oedipal betrayal staining all my shadows, ill, forgotten, miserable, shivering from frostbite and fright, contorting inside bed sheets doused in fever, in tears.

In light of these atrocious and sudden strikes, veritable alarm signals, the genial embraces that double them suddenly seem suspect to me, and my most urgent necessity alike, projecting the theoretical void that unravels me and paralyzes all of my mental activities, to create around me a corresponding void which, despite its suffocating and unendurable aspect, eliminates the cloying admixture of good and evil furnished to me by the exterior world and which for me is the image of the Oedipal double and the most sinister mask of error. I can't bear the thought that after being struck by surprise, I should seek, by virtue of inertia and mechanical self-conservation, refuge in the arms of the lover, because the arms of the lover are guilty of that strike as well, and, if their super-determinant complicity has not been visible enough to me, it becomes so the moment we take refuge in these arms, because of the unforgivable error we commit in idealizing love's reality by superimposing it upon the most apparent and confusion-engendering realities of the external world, upon that most alien to the objective reality of love. In order to avoid the flight into a favorable illusion after contact with an unfavorable reality, I prefer to unmask the partial complicity and causality of the lover, rather than to idealize her compensatory charms, I prefer to take my desperation to its ultimate consequence (which must contain within it a favorable dialectical exit), I prefer it to a refuge in which under the best of circumstances my wounds are dressed and my pus is disinfected, if the adorable lapse of my lover doesn't intervene by causing her to confuse the bottle of iodine with that of poison.

It is enough to walk around in a dark room in search of a photograph or a handkerchief and collide accidentally into something or scratch myself or prick my finger lightly with a needle in order to engage, through the mystery of the drop of blood on the tip of my finger, the most distant erotic causalities and the most unlikely astrological, social and universal collaborations. I know the extent that the causal projection of my despair upon absolutely every single person who surrounds me might suggest a case of persecution mania in its acute phase but the psychological association of my demeanor will not succeed in abolishing the objective significance which I accord to paranoia, especially for the purpose of denouncing those loved ones surrounding me, I have at my disposal an entire arsenal of objective analysis, convincing in itself, without the need of the maniacal subjective support of my own person.

In fact I don't have a lot of interest in whether my accusations are legitimate or not; what interests me most and what I feel as an irresistible necessity is for the theoretical void within me to be sustained by my external actions all the way into their very fibers, to the point of the most absurd consequences, indifferent to the vagrant anguish which I provoke inside myself and indifferent to the apparent self-flagellating masochistization implied in it; what concerns me is the veritable pleasure which only a veritable position on the theoretical plane endlessly assures me, the insignificant pleasures and the insignificant sadomasochistic anguishes being no more than negligible to me in the context of this attraction to an unforeseen, invented and vehement—but always present—pleasure, in the context of this visionary presence in a more certain reality.

In order for my theoretical errors (unknown to me but certain), which recently have caused me to be so vulnerable vis-à-vis the external world's incessant sadism, in order for them to be dialectically toppled, I am being offered the first fundamentally synthetic escape route (actually fundamentally synthetic for all revolutionary spirits) in the tendency to maintain myself along the same unsteady equilibrium of negation and negation's negation that causes us to be in incessant agreement with our own selves. The theoretical void that I feel, almost like a pneumatic physical reality, forces me to send to each and every person who loves me parting letters in which I unmask their hatred, these persons being filled with the same latent characteristics of hatred that the rest of the external world has for me, the physical separation from these persons being for me not only a reconciliation of the practical tensions with the theoretical ones but also an elementary measure of security. For a few days now I have not seen anyone, and if the absence of the woman I love, of the human warmth and voice, produces in me an anxiety of the highest level, on the other hand, my self-enforced solitude—practical, systematic, predatory—aggravates beyond limits my immense and immeasurable desperation.

I don't know what to do. After I have done everything I could in order to be in agreement with myself (the same way that the bullet is in agreement with the blood it spills), after I have dodged all the snares the external world set for me in its Oedipal perfidy set on counterveiling the immense indecency it perpetrated upon me, after I have superimposed my theoretical and desperate void, reflecting it as in a mirror's mirror into my deserted life, into my interrupted gestures, into my tormenting and prolonged insomnias, my perpetual agony, I can't see what I might do with my persona, so frozen with desperation, if I didn't place it face-to-face with death, because only death can express in its obscurantist and fatal tongue, the real death that consumes me, that permeates me, that obscures me to the point of disappearance.

What directs me towards death as if towards a near-logical conclusion of my absolute negation, comes up against its quantitative obstacle, in which I recognize as in the rotten entrails of a pig, the absolute triviality of its Creator and his simple-minded, utilitarian and ignoble imagination. This unrefined death, natural and traumatic, even more castrating in its nature than the birth it reflects and completes, seems to me unacceptable, not only because it takes the concept of castration to the demoniacal extreme of our complete physical dissolution, but also because this one-dimensional death doesn't correspond to the dialectical leaps that direct us towards it, its fixed, mechanical absolute opposite, making the free expression of our necessities impossible, there, where causes and effects are prevented from exchanging destinies among themselves. The continual presence of death in the funereal obscurity of my being will never assume, on the plane of necessity, the paralyzing and idealist aspects of the death invented by the Creator, this structurally religious death, like the current life it will disappear together with the rest of the obstacle posed by the external life, together with the ultimate repression. The death that I contain as a necessity, as desperation's safety valve, as a retort to love and hate, as an extension of my being within my own contradictions, I recognize it in the anxious and lubricious aspects it takes on in dreams, in toxicomania, in catalepsy, in ambulatory automatism, in other hundreds of thousands of instances of cohabitation of man and his shadow, of shadow and its flame, I recognized it in the masked necrophilia I nurse, forcing my lover to affect a glacial passivity during the sexual act, I recognize it even in the mechanical act of slumber, of swooning, of the epileptic seizure, but never will I recognize, not even in my most self-flagellant reveries, the objectivity of this sinister phenomenon which monotonizes us, which replicates us, which exterminates us as if we were hundreds of thousands of times the millenary victim of a senile and cynical monomaniac. The distension of this necessary death which must not traumatically contradict life and which must resolve it in the sense of an uninterrupted negation in which reciprocity and causal reversal must be possible, the distension of this objective death as a retort to my objective life, incessantly penetrated by the incandescent objectivity of my love-affairs, forces me today to traverse a terrain of desolation without margins, of moral catalepsy taken to the point of theoretical void and insoluble despair of a macabre and revolutionary kind, forces me to aggravate this terrain of acute irritation, exasperating it to the point of its impossible negation, and to the point of the exasperating negation of the impossible, where death, in order to be devoured like a woman, abandons its traumatic qualities and becomes consumed, qualitatively, thaumaturgically and adorably, in *humor*.

Utilizing the same ciphered signs of our interior cipher, resorting again to the Irrespirable Triangle which is the Artifice, to the Woman with a Thousand Furs, which is automatism, to the Double Heart which is the Inspired Somnambulism, and to the Great, Unequaled Whale which is the Simulacrum, I have been performing for the last few days repeated suicide attempts, which are not only a logical consequence of deception, of my subjective saturation and despair, but also my first real and virtual victory against the Absolute General Paralytic which is death.

I can no longer bear this life full of privation.[1]

1. Letter left on the table during the first suicide attempt.

I. I attempt to commit suicide by strangulation with the aid of a necktie, which I fasten to the door handle. I had left upon the table a letter whose content seemed irresistibly comical to me: *I can no longer bear this life full of privation.*

The absence of any perceptible motive, reducible to a general formula, acknowledges in my suicide "due to poverty" a crudely economical facsimile, but one still full of charm. Out of all of the apparent motives invoked by suicides, this one always provoked in me a singular repulsion because of its slavish, masochistic, and plainly counter-revolutionary character. I couldn't have left a more misleading letter on top of my corpse; the word privation in particular assumes all of the languor and beatitude of the miserable. Although it sticks out its tongue with an involuntary, belligerent, and satirical inclination, my nouveau-cadaver ascends, courtesy of this letter, the first step on the social ladder.

A dizziness in which I recognize my passion for intoxication, for suffocation, for the disappearance of certitude. I raise my hands to my neck probably in order to prevent strangulation, but my gesture is so violent that it appears as wanting to reinforce it, to duplicate it.

I haven't worn a tie in eight years.

(Note taken down at the time)

Violeme fnystherisant
toi, l'oubrée

c'est le sang noir

et l'oubli

c' est le desir d'oublier tout

sauf le desir

Causes of my death not to be looked for;
there are no guilty, not even myself.
I forsake life without any regrets.
I ask for restraint at my funeral,
cremation if possible.
Flowers for me not to be brought.[2]

2. Letter left on the table during the second suicide attempt.

II. I have never before been so disturbed by my eyes, by my mouth, by the pallor that enshrouds my face. I am so aroused that I constantly oscillate between temptations to commit suicide and to masturbate. The graphomania I scribble on the mirror with my left hand while with my right I squeeze the trigger of the revolver pressed against my temple, seems to be written by someone else, by a shadow or other mirror.

Probably contributing towards this state of arousal, I must not forget to mention, is the farewell letter left upon the table. The spirit of hygiene and sobriety that animates it, its imprecise and mechanical materialism of a bourgeois and elementary nature recalling the general posture vis-à-vis all the conquests of civilization (radio, aviation, television) and especially its utilitarian common sense ("flowers not to be brought") disturbs my revolutionary theoretical position through its grotesque antagonisms and eroticizes it to the utmost.

My brain hurts.

(Note taken down at the time)

Tes larmes ton parfum, ton desespoir mon supplice

O, my darling![3]

---

3. Letter left on the table during the third suicide attempt.

III. The prolonged and intentionally theatrical pronunciation of the letter O, followed by the adored name of the lover, is enough to express the latent melancholy of my love anesthetizing my fury, clamorous despair, and exhibitionism, replacing them with a deaf and tacit cruelty as in the vampirical and catalepsy-producing exercises found in the love-life of carnivorous plants.

In spite of all this I furiously plunge the knife into my heart.

The graphomania scribbled with my left hand while the right holds the knife, preserves the latent melancholy of love, preserves and suckles it.

(Note taken down at the time)

La fatalité m'atire
par son inexistence
par ses grands
Jeux noirs

A nervous illness never incurable never which never tortures
me for many years never forces me never to end my days.
I pay never with my life for the sins of my parents never my
heredity never was burden. If I never did no one wrong I never
ask for forgiveness.[4]

4. Letter left on the table during the fourth suicide attempt.

IV. I drink the contents of a bottle filled with poison, the same one that served, in minor doses, to soothe my abdominal crises. I writhe on the ground with my grimacing face and have no idea why my mind fills with a few anxious scenes from the animal domain: worms of various lengths, poisonous snakes, a cat kicked to death, dogs in heat, a horse stabbed in rage, and only at the end appears the image of the woman I saw last year, the woman I saw writhing on the floor of her garret in a full crisis of hysteria, projecting at least as powerfully as an earthquake, the image of unleashed love.

"Fatality," the first word written a few seconds after I swallowed the poison, is intrinsically much more connected to the woman's fatality (hysteria) than to the destiny's fatality as opposed to its determinism, while "inexistence" is a compromise between the fatality's concrete unreality and the concrete unreality of that woman who is late, who does not show up and ingests me through her huge black eyes until I disappear.

The stereotypical repetition of the word never in my good-bye letter completes the hysterical content that I accord to the idea of fatality and inexistence. The metaphysical content of these ideas, no less compromised than nothingness, the absolute, the infinite, etc., acquire an unique materiality if we allow it to be convulsed by the great hysteria and if we savor its mystifying and cold precipitates through "humor."

(Note taken down at the time)

Je suis inspiré par
un grand oiseau rouge
qui déchire deux grands
oiseaux pourris qui déchirent
à leur tour un grand
piano à queue

If it is true, as the errors claim, that after death man continues a phantomatic existence, I will let you know. If you do not hear from me for one month, you will know that death is no different than the putrefaction of an onion, a chair, a hat.

I commit suicide out of disgust.[5]

5. Letter left on the table during the fifth suicide attempt.

V. I attempt suicide via the voluntary obstruction of breath. Because of the gigantic effort I make to throttle myself (not to throttle myself), the writing of this text becomes an ordeal. The disordered burning that takes place inside my body and which I sense in my temples and my heart, which beats faster and faster, puts me in a mechanical state similar to the one preceding arousal (though I feel no erotic excitement manifest). The attempt to commit suicide through the impossible produces in me a veritable mental euphoria, the physical arousal proceeding only after I return to the anterior respiratory condition, corresponding to an actual intrauterine return. The toppling, not merely nostalgic or sublimated, of the natal trauma aided by the simulacrum is all the more visible as my suicide attempt through the impossible is no more than a replay of the multiple intrauterine returns realized in childhood through the game in which we compete to see who can hold his breath the longest. Bounding over the sado-anal signification, secondary in nature, intermediary and contained, the suicide attempt through the impossible has for me a colossal theoretical value, because of my constant attempts, practical and theoretical, of toppling, through the impossible, the natal trauma, whose fatality seems to me inadmissible, because it is non-dialectical, and as long as I continue to take a stance against pain, I will persist in seeing in it a grave, monstrous, most oppressive error.

My farewell letter does no more than prolong this same idea of the intrauterine return, but this time in its nostalgic sense. The superimposition of my attraction to death over that of the intrauterine, the way it emerges from my farewell letter, is too simplistic not to be obscurantist, not to be traumatic in itself.

The graphomania scribbled while making a contradictory double effort of will (to throttle myself and not to throttle myself) is indeed a corporal struggle with my own self, with death and the writing mania, a supreme act of rape exercised against the blind forces of darkness; written in a state of especially exceptional physical agitation, its correct and serene calligraphic form remains an enigma to me.

(Note taken down at the time)

APPENDIX

In order to avoid the flight into a favorable illusion after contact with an unfavorable reality, I prefer to unmask the partial complicity and causality of the lover, rather than to idealize her compensatory charms, I prefer to take my desperation to its ultimate consequence (which must contain within it a favorable dialectical exit), I prefer it to a refuge in which...

Indeed, a favorable solution cannot be extracted except from inside an extreme position, where the dialectical confrontation is taken to the point of mania, to the most improbable and most delirious verification. Any attempt to save myself from the ruins by grabbing onto a beam or the foot of one of the wounded would be fatal. The ruination of the ruins offered me the means of traversing the ruins unscathed and only the perpetual dynamiting of the tumbling edifice had the force to assure my escape from the ferocious teeth of negation, not as a cripple, happy to have at least escaped with his life, but as an infinitely causal conclusion of it, confirming anew the validity of a theory and the concrete nature of revolution.

Rejecting any compromising solution dependent upon economy of effort and unilateral preservation instinct, bringing even unto the black barriers of death my repulsion for the pleasure-pain duality, from which humans chose with traditional candor their pleasant stupidity, their filth: it is good, as good as it can get, I allow myself to be devoured by pain with the same fervor I direct myself towards that which is inexpressible in pleasure. In agreement with my theoretical precipitates, this apparent catastrophe in the realm of pain sustains my constant appetite for the objective reality of pleasure, verifiable only through the objective surprise it promises us, current pleasures, accessible, alternating with displeasure and doubled by the reverse side of the picture, being for me the direct expression of unhappiness, of Sunday, of recreation, of the wedding, and everything else that makes a burden out of the joys and sorrows of this slave world.

I prefer death, a thousand times death, to the inexact pleasure provoked by daylight upon exiting the mine; to the infirm joy of moving about at will after a long malady; of the first party, the first pair of long trousers, the first cigarette, the first journey, the first love in our biography. These apparent pleasures, provoked by the historical accident of a privation and the error of a temporal monotony, these delights of the weary lying on their beds, on any beds, these orgies of the miserable wretch who is granted food to eat, who will eat anything, all these disproportions, unjustified in the affective economy of the oppressed, thwart the veritable objectification of pleasure, and throttles, inside the theatre of an eternal retaliation, the incessant surpassing of necessity.

The apparent shipwreck of my non-Oedipal activities aimed to toss me alive to the claws of a scattered error of thinking that causes the most agitated of revolutionaries to affirm: in a society divided by the class system, love is not attainable, being the automatic support for its tyranny or subliminal evasions, while forgetting that the single possibility of preserving the insurrectional efficacy of such an affirmation is the immediate negation of the horror it contains and its paralyzing dominance. Everything is unattainable in the odious society divided by the class system, everything including love, including breath, dreams, smiles, embraces, everything outside the incandescent reality of becoming. To manifestly recognize our powerlessness, no matter how migratory, before the obstacle, knowing that the biological rhythms of humans may differ from the rhythm of historical liberation, would bring along with it the idealization of the revolution and would thwart the material discernment between relative-absolute reality of desire and the relative-absolute reality of its realization. The relative-absolute realization of desire in the middle of contemporary society, *surprised at the border of its own contradictions,* is the only means to get in contact with the classless society, and this first dose of objective freedom that we wrench through the systematic invocation of fortuitous chance, through the sustained provocation of our latent mediumistic attributes, through the forced determination of the revolutionary determinants, and through a perpetual breach into the exterior world, causes us to reject our actual incarceration with the kind of hatred that only our demented love can equal.

Under threat that my constant dialectical despair before love may transmute into a formal and logical despair, connected to the presence of obstacle, I allow myself to be directed by my own negations wherever I may be, in any snare or trap of contraries, through the darkest and most tortuous corridors of risk, the risk of losing not only my theoretical lucidity, but even the most elementary physical support. Only by aggravating historical pessimism vis-à-vis obstacle to the point of paranoid dynamism, only by despairing despair and maintaining it with fervor in a position of unlimited pessimism, pessimistic but permanently voluptuous vis-à-vis love, my non-Oedipal activity of today, only a few months after the disorienting confrontation between two contrary dialectics, makes contact with, in its revolutionary journey towards the forced objectivity of love, slashes of reality which even non-Oedipus won't dare dream of.

Wresting man's heart from the complexual absolute in which its throbbing was fixed, returning it, still living, to its own dialectical leaps, the non-Oedipal position projects for the first time in the form of human behavior that sumptuous liberation of matter from its petrified three-dimensionality, the theoretical and experimental rediscovery of the universe, which the new relativistic problem furnishes us with, and which non-Oedipus reflects theoretically and experimentally in the field of love, constitutes at present a veritable infusion of the real, an unsuspected capture and devouring of the real, and implicitly the denunciation of a symmetrical world, mechanical, positive, formal, regressive, enslaving, elementary, spatial and corpuscular, a world that supports biology, society, and the universe of my contemporaries. Exchanging the particular between them, the crystals and their uninterrupted assault on nature, preserving on the lips the indecipherable kiss of the quanta and the inexpressible, time-space and non-Oedipus follow through the same curious and priapic spyglass the spectral constellation of exceeding the human.

THE
PRAYING
MANTIS
APPRAISED

THE FENCING FOIL WITH
CIRCLES UNDER ITS EYELIDS

Cadaverous in my mantle studded with combs that still retain the hairs of this woman I pursue, I pursue her on a street on which nothing is absent save inhabitants and doors. Solitary on the streets of this city camouflaged by lianas, disinterred by my eyeball, my eyeball putrid like the sneering of a corpse, the woman I pursue fumbles near my shoulder and a slender wind flutters through my fingers. I inspire the air from metal canisters whose inner walls gargle like organs. And on my minutely pressing-forward shoulder blades, another organ, its keys depressed by vultures and bats, its note-score sliced on slightly charred parchment upon which a damsel from the ninth century set her cheekbones on a scorching afternoon. Pushing, with palms thrust forth, the gloom through which I wander with the aid of a single lantern, this woman, half leopard, which I palpate next to me like tree bark. Each sector of the route I roam is layered with corpses, dog corpses engorged by cat corpses, like an opened mouth alive with an abundance of butterfly corpses. A single apricot tree blooms in the entire landscape and it is I. Megalomaniac like any hand inside a glove, I am afflicted by belts that drag me backwards, wet ropes ravishing my hair, lungs that I wear, out of bravado, pinned to my chest. I stroll about posing such forced spontaneity that if I were merely a spectator I would call myself a statue. To be your own statue, to step up on your own plinth as you would ascend a formal carriage, and to cross the cityscape over which you attempted so many times to scrawl with fingers of ash: *the fencing foil with circles under its eyelids*. I am moved to tears by my metallic gaze and the corpse's sneer I sport upon my lips. I am calm and more certain of myself than if I had swallowed a lactating cow. I stroll about with a step of marble, listen with an ear of drums, I scrutinize with an eyeball shooting out of the middle of my forehead like a tree that would tint its leaves its own favorite hue. I challenge myself to a game of marbles, which I extract from my pockets and I am always the winner. Chance is on my side incessantly. It is fruitless to calculate probabilities in matters of chance, chance is nothing if not auspicious. The malleability of my cranial bones causes my nights spent outdoors to wear an entrancing gauze, sleeping as I do on one temple as I would upon a pillow. The sky displays exactly the stars I require, I am familiar with their number, I determine it myself. One plunges down and I snatch it. A bird (the corpse of a bird) lands upon my shoulder blades.

THE CARNATION'S MISFORTUNES

The next day the ocean seemed more enrapturing to me than an operating table. With frowning locks flung over my shoulders, this outmoded mantle from which I never separate, I board this raft without first forgetting to leave upon the shore the two oars, futile in my thirst for carnations, in my hunger to have been tenebrous. Prone upon my spine with my hunting dog supine upon my chest, I gaze with nostalgia into the sky, enumerating unto thousands the stars, the moon, the wolf's lair, the vermilion, the Danube, the plague, etc. Over my brow creeps the slashing lip of a saber and two drops of blood trickle on my cheek recalling the illustrious inner episodes I am about to intersect like the mysteries of a circus. Monocle fitted to my eyeball, mustache twisting with panache, I stride forth, reckless and virile, spellbound and entrancing, slurping with swelling cheeks this magnificent poisonous broth which is our internal life. You are a fawn stalked by the swift hunter within me, yes, you! the most enrapturing idol I ever pursued, you who transforms the outer world into the unsurpassed ideal of our internal murmur. With temples bonded one to the other and both bonded to a marble statue, we roam across a sensate alley and our footsteps disinter cities, rivers, hawks.

I hoist you upon my shoulder as one would hoist a horseman, and with palm above the eyelashes in mimic of the eaves I spy upon the sap surging up through distant trees, murder a bird in flight, darken the horizon. Your lashes transmute into a pillow of tresses into which I plunge my fingers all the way up to the elbow as I might bathe them in a cauldron of blood and haul out a silver battle helmet missing only the skullcap. O! enrapturing idol with the unruffled breath of snails, with the clamor of bones malefic like a shiver of fright, I carry you in my arms like a cauldron for bathing cobras. How tender are the unconcealed symbols and how many tears I would shed over the tiny superstitions misplaced in tiny provincial towns if my eyeball didn't boast of a retina that could spin an image about nine times. A limestone retina where they dump empty sardine cans left behind by negligent tourists. Inebriated to the point of vertigo by the spin of this misleading spectacle, where the entrancing and odious, tact and impudence, transgression and atonement assemble in your smile, the retina transmutes into a green mustang with mirroring knees. I myself a mirror, a horseshoe mirror, and your trotting canter appears, perused across the glowing surface of a mountain lake. Massive rocks engorge us at the precise instant I tether my ascot. O, the tenderness of unconcealed symbols, o! o! O, my idol, o! the unconcealed symbol of this idol, the symbol's symbol, inflaming reality's realities, while the unreal, entrancing as a vampire, beckons me with secret ciphers, from without and within, with hand-in-glove or merely with her skeleton.

THE PRAYING MANTIS APPRAISED

The seemingly uncanny phenomena that I suspect are unfolding within the interior of an orange placed upon a metal plate reveals to me my own mental life, as if a spontaneous reversal occurs, long yearned for, between the contents of this orange and my own cranial crate. It is a crate that thinks this orange, I discern the tenebrous circumvolutions obscuring even more the questions being asked there, under this neutral and discolored yellow rind, the only uncertain aspect in this hallucinatory blend of reality. As beneath the skull trickles a turbid juice, scented with an imaginal Mediterranean, simulated, my nostrils trepidate like a bird from which the eyeballs have been removed, these eyeballs so disagreeable, so irremediably riveting. The mental life of a fruit, the vegetal history of thought! There is nothing that seems to me more certain than this variety of momentary solutions opening for us into infinity by the adventure of thinking. Intermediary solutions, swift, fluctuating, yet each time flawless and utterly satisfying. Desire awakened with a tense fury, fastidious, out of its provisional fulfillment. This permanent condition of provisional plight of solutions populates the world which I inhabit with veils, bats and abandoned statues that my eyeballs, aroused to the level of clairvoyance, track with eyelids forced open in order not to give the appearance of being shut.

    I experience the sentiments of a mathematician who bears a grudge against the cipher, axioms are corpses we ignore almost out of spite while sophistry, propped up on shoulders

cloaked by a mantle crisscrossed on sabers, stages for its pre-
miere a stately entrance in our mental life. Sophistry and the
arbitrary, the shadow and the tracks of footsteps on sand, the
ephemeral plight of childhood's soap bubbles, a mask of dia-
monds draped over a face, mask which, from the viewpoint of
the long-sought truth, I prefer over the concealed visage itself,
the marvelous being a method far more rigorously exacting in
this field of research which is the human being itself, all these
uncertain and intentionally frail footbridges that we toss from
one phenomenon to another, and inside the same phenome-
non I infuse the foot which traverses them with the natural
certainty, the unnatural as well, of a sleepwalking stroll, the
certitude, real and imaginal, of a woman in a state of catalepsy.
I know of no opium to oppugn the dialectically violent trope
"the opium of the people," utilized by Lenin in a pejorative
mode when he attempts to wrench the mask off the annihi-
latingly cretinizing intentions of religion, than this hallucina-
tory product employed to serve the revolution. This trans-
figuration of our room into an opium den contributes in a
systematic manner to the acceleration, the exacerbation and
inflammation of the actual conflict within humanity.

This explanation of a social aspect, which might imply my
tendency to justify certain personal inclinations, does not ex-
haust the unlimited trust I accord to each convulsive activity;
at first view incomprehensible, not yet substantiated. The
world inside the human being, inside objects, will continue to
provoke in me the same perplexed and bewildered state, un-
breathable and faintly demented, occasioned in me by the de-
scription staged upon this planet's school benches, employing
an image-cliché perpetrated to us in preference of the earth's
living crust with its oceans, volcanoes and immense moun-
tains, a thin orange rind. The orange, around which, ever since
then, spin all the comets of the questions I am being asked

(the orange having long ceased for me to be an image-cliché, even less so the idea of the orange alone) is just as juicy, just as fragrant as any orange placed carelessly next to a knife. I deliver this orange to my lips and each time I do I have the sensation of that Romanian peasant who, having been handed a bar of soap for the first time, did not suspect that it would serve him for any other purpose than as something to eat. I squeeze its juice between my teeth and foam of the uncertain hue and consistency of your hair fills my mouth. Any attempt to externalize this sensation, as pleasant as a kiss, gives birth to a facile swarm of ambiguities. I eat a bar of soap in the same manner I eat your hair, in the same manner I breathe in your mouth when my fingers search your skin in the dark as though I were searching for the lamp's switch. I ate a lamp maybe, maybe I devoured the praying mantis I appraised, maybe I ate nothing but your inedible image, your image reflected in my palm which I hold slightly at a slope above your head in order to divine your murmurous undertow but not your existence. It is an orange, my palm circular as a head, which I place under your foot to hoist you in the air in mimic of acrobats and your chiromantic strolls along my life line and love line are the only realities that I do not like to doubt. I adore flesh and shadow and easily exchange this entrancing lover for the tracks she leaves in the sand like hieroglyphs. Lounging at the foot of my enrapturing lover, I do not discern that between us stretches a field, a railroad, a universe. Solitary in my room like a smoker of opium inhaling your flesh from afar, your flowering shoulders, your lips from which escapes a bird, a veil, I ask you as I would ask a hairbrush: are you dead? have you been born? have I met you? am I going to meet you?

My answer does not depend upon your answer: I am not alone.

THE VOLCANOES INSIDE VEGETABLES

A canoe made of hair, it seems to me, with soft paddles, gelatinous, like sea animals, beneath which a woman, entirely of crystal, rolls a ball bearing from one lip to the other, is the image-archetype of pollution. During one of my pollutical nights, unhappily so rare, when the poplars lining up before my domicile adopted a compulsively fastidious aspect in their evening frocks, and the violins in my gestures assumed a discreet sound like torture instruments, my imperiously intrepid position vis-à-vis amorous rendezvous seemed to me a disquieting distortion of metallic facial wrinkles on a metallic face affixed to a body that accents only its rigid and osseous sections, neglecting the passive-voluptuous subtlety and incertitude of its weft, its lungs, the predilection accorded the skeleton in our current amorous life replacing for me in demoralizing fashion the popular image of death. I don't know to what measure the castration complex can be introduced into an enterprise, be it sentimental and empathetic like this one, where the denunciation of a massive action on the erotic plane is tested. I understand that sadomasochistic game-playing transforms much of the schematic aspect under which I expound these matters, but what I wish to affirm essentially is that the male and its fabricated rigidity fills the eyeball that observes it from without with nausea. I am disgusted by the darling violence of the male, and this disgust entails, with more authority than at any other time, a certain objectivity, because the unpleasant sentiment to which I am subjected finds me inside the phenomenon, finds myself personally occupying in the realm of the amorous a faintly sadistic position.

The disdain towards the petty histrionics that accompany practically every moment in this stripe of active pursuits when sadism is not enacted to its morbid degrees, but is sustained rather within general, theatrical contours, its gesticulations adopting a mannered path, causes me to envy the essentially apparent passivity of the female, because I find it more spontaneous in its reactions, more revealing, more vibrant. I am aware of the risk I take in terms of consequences in the analytical realm that such affirmations may provoke and I believe I may lighten up the workload of the eventual psychoanalyst if I remind him of the extensive masturbatory exercises to which the author of these lines dedicated himself during his adolescence, exercises which still, from time to time, hold him in their allure as the scene of the crime does the criminal. I confess however that my psychoanalyst's file holds little interest for me because my personal position within a complex cannot exhaust assessments of a general character provoked by the examination of this erotic spectacle where one of the actors is (in)vested in a rigid mantle of bones while the other is a nerve severed with a saw. In order for the male's bones to crack, in order for the marrow within them to spill out like lava, they would need to be invested with the nebulous and satanic consistency of a Marquis de Sade. It seems to me that it is not necessary to take passivity to its ultimate end in order for it to become entirely sensitized. I see myself at the roots of a tree taken by surprise by a woman in a red blouse glued to her skin, with long black hair strewn in disarray over her shoulders, eyes like burnt brush. The caresses or the bites of this woman are just as voluptuous to me, the element of surprise containing in its fulgurance a state of panic-arousal, capable of transcending any previous commonplace state. This horrific woman, if she is not sadistic in the extreme, if she does not arouse me to envision her awakening the next day in a distant forest next to my corpse, with her hands stained with blood, is frustrated in her vibrancy of pitch, in her howl of ash. I place my lips upon the eyeballs of this incomplete and minor image of passivity, flowers with irresolute butterflies swarming around them like vultures. In my bedsheets with drawn curtains, the circles round the eyeballs I touch are silent electrical doorbells. The pores are at hand, I am a rubber ball, the hair is far above the head, my eyeball's tongue the mouth of this unborn woman. A tree on my forehead, transparent and somewhat sparrow, its leaves dropping loose throughout the room, o! what an odd spring. A thick smoke suffuses my arm and thin trails as if from a cigarette exude from my fingers, their nails surprisingly stained a promiscuous yellow. With these stained fingers I leaf through a papyrus, an apricot. Nights fall too quickly in my house for dawn ever to break. The rains within are quick, walls sway, weeds and canoes float upon my lips, perhaps they are my words. My words bite your thighs, it is as though my teeth were written. It is a delirious calligraphy, to be studied today by tomorrow's graphology inside pyramids under an immense block of ice growing in the middle of the desert like a miracle. The mysterious calligraphy of illiterates where images seem closer to objects that have not been invented yet, the simulated calligraphy of illiterates. I open you up like a horse and look inside for the bridle bit, forgetting you already hold it between your teeth. Night falls again, it is night incessantly. It is the witching hour, permanently bewitching, where the consistency of your being is far more certain than flesh, your bewitching flesh, permanently bewitching. I caress your ectoplasm as I would a shark. I sip you from tall beakers of crystal propped upon a living frog's leg. I invite you, I shout you, I bestow a name upon you, any name. Fog, hair, a mask of quicksilver over your eyes, the vegetables from our virtual gestures, the tiger sleeping on our voice and the salutation we perform reciprocally for one another from the window, lifting from our shoulders with two fingers our skulls like a hat while the trains transporting us in two opposite directions crash into one another like a snowflake.

MINERAL O! STATUE OF DESIRE

I stroll along a rampart clutching under my arm a length of fog from which the belly of a woman, the lips of a woman on the belly of this woman are glued to the overcast forehead of a thinker from the past century pierced in succession by a saber, a thunderbolt, a flock, a cosmos of birds. This rampart, I don't know by what sort of miracle appositioned parallel to the ocean, I don't know which game of chance, spewing from me and crashing against the great ground swell hailing from afar accompanies my strolls, spawning the suspicion that I am in the midst of a city that has been recently excavated, perhaps a city at the bottom of the ocean, perhaps a city inside a porpoise. The hat upon my head is deliberately outmoded, I wear an opiate eyeball, wayward, a lean mouth beneath a sumptuous mustache, enshrouded entirely in velvet, my simultaneous approach to this ruined rampart and to the ocean provokes me to tears. I cried silently as during a slumber in which too many things are revealed to you at once, the tears streaming down my face in order to complete this landscape which is truly a dream landscape where I like to always stay awake.

My legs are now spiderwebs and the sand beneath them does not even retain the traces of my steps, as light as breathing. It is more like a murmur, my stroll, a zephyr. In exchange my head leaves visible tracks and once home how exuberantly I follow through a crack in the window the succession of headprints extending out into the distance and anchoring the ocean to me. Yesterday I went out but not before I put on a very tall opera hat simply for the satisfaction of subsequently spying on the incessant succession of opera hats tumbling into the surf. Have I disposed of myself? I doubt it, having opted for this leisurely mode of disposal labeled life I can't conceive why my existence should have concluded yesterday. But perhaps my life is one thing while what came to pass surpasses what is surmised through the antinomy of life and death. I am entirely ridiculous. I should paint a sparrow on my face and hook to my buttonhole the map of a country that has passed into obscurity. Progressively more ridiculous. I twist on the faucet in the bathtub, (yes, I do have a bathtub!), I shut the window, I eat a plum, I stare in the mirror, I organize my mustache. The mustache once again? How many more times do I need to bite from this fruit full of worms in order to be able to taste what has been labeled life's experience, in order to be no longer bewitched by the charm of its cadaverous putrefaction? The decadence of each gesture I execute like a death sentence and the aura that surrounds my head each time I think about corpses, about wax figures, about ruins, manuscripts half devastated by arson, about a spoon between the fingers of a woman putrefying leisurely on its journey to the mouth, about movements captured in slow-motion in old movies, but preeminently about mustaches, the mustaches of men at the turn of the century, provoke me to peruse the things that surround me with an eyeball that presupposes itself perused, with an eyeball of stone pursued by a stone of flesh and, impervious to how minuscule and how relative this casually passive and easily violated position might be, I can't deprive myself of its morbid charm. I would like to possess the philosopher's stone and transmute lead to gold. I would like to murder a child and spare the life of a butterfly.

My stroll to the Unending along the rampart in ruins would perhaps appear less perplexing if it were discovered that in this grand metropolis sufficient amounts of the velvety blood of oppression had been spilled. I am not accountable if the human being provokes me to disgust while the mouse doesn't (if I were to discover a mouse in my soup tureen, it would be far more palatable than a human being) with my head propped up on a pillow of bats, reclining upon a grassy plain of carnivorous plants, next to a woman whose lips are bloody suction cups, whose hair is obsidian fulguration, whose fingers are plush pile shelters for slumbering snails, while eavesdropping on the distant baying of wolves, slumber would apprehend me imperceptibly like the swaying of a riverbed. I fall into slumber with open eyeballs, omniscient as antennas trained upon wherever bedsheets of virginal aspect erupt unexpectedly like a volcano. The more alluring the oscillation between two complementary colors appears to me, the more I discern that their encounter in a third color is merely provisional and that in their secret underbelly, in their unconfessed grottoes strolls this ungraspable phantom, white in its mantle of tears. Out of a parallel impulse, deviant to a degree, I find black alluring, I find this frogman's diving suit alluring, this powdered mascara, and the inexistence of this color in nature provokes me to ponder a long procession of cowls, a chamber inside a castle with cloistered windows, a fountain reflecting stars during the course of the day, provokes me to even ponder butterflies.

"Combien de fois, au moment de mettre du bleu, j'ai constaté que j'en manquais! Alors j'ai pris du rouge et je l'ai mis à la place du bleu." (Picasso). If I were a painter I would paint the trees in my landscape black and my eyeball green. This exchange of colors between the eyeball that sees and the thing that is seen, apart from the theoretical value that I accord it in this grim antinomy where it inhabits the region of synthesis, it corresponds on the lyric plane to the pallor of a human being that

has been staring at its likeness for at least the last few tens of centuries in the glimmer of liquid, this narcissistic drama becoming, in the sense that the human being ceased to see only itself in this magical mirror, all the more convoluted in contemporary lyricism. This transposition of colors or fevers between the eyeball that sees and the thing that it sees is more alluring, it seems to me, than two starving jackals that defer to one another the privilege to the next bite. Leaning over this magic looking glass the size of my eyeball and of the universe, I purposefully mistake my own unease for that of humanity and find it unnecessary to keep in mind a sense of proportion when I ponder the passage of the woman who enraptures me through my chamber and that of a comet allured by the cosmic lure of the earth. And I commit no abuse of metaphor when I liken the sliding of the strata instigating earthquakes with the fingers she places over my forehead under which the blood begins to quicken its pace, under which the blood begins to boil.

It is time that this man makes an exit, this being with his head balanced on a scale-tally and eyeball anchored to a caliper, preserved like sacred relics in a Paris crypt, repulsive fetish of the Occident. I breathe in the hair of the woman who enraptures me and forest fills my lungs, I seize her lips between my lips and evening envelops me. In her vestment woven of wind and fog this enrapturing lover hurls me a kiss from her balcony without resorting to the intermediary of a rose. I carry her in my arms along this rampart parallel to the ocean and while it disintegrates to ruin our fingers sprout with leaves, birds warble, ivy soars, our tongues coil around a splinter of coal, we shatter it with our teeth gleaming in sudden alabaster white.

Could it be a simple exit from the kingdom, after this sorrowful attempt to abandon the species, the repulsive human species, are we nearing the mineral realm, the vegetable, like those flying fish, a tryst of water and air? Water and fire, could it be that they have chosen us? Are we their nuptial bed, the gaming-table of the elements, this gamble where life itself is the wager? Shall we hurl ourselves into the ocean, shall we hurl ourselves into the rampart? Shall we sink our teeth into rocks, waves, shadows, roses? Shall we clothe ourselves in ruins and wrap into our evening dress this heap of sand? Will your satin slipper fit the sand's foot? Do you think the phantoms who inhabit beyond the rampart, the phantoms we await, will come? Are we phantom enough?

THE FORESHADOWED CASTLE

The phantastic bird, who is not yet named, whose form has not even been vaguely determined, whose mission, whose flight, whose song, whose transparency is not yet known, this phantastic bird erupting from dreams before you even acknowledge its being, I carry this bird unendingly on my shoulder with the disconsolate feeling that I have trained my eyeballs to glance in the other direction while behind me unfurls, silently, the most significant portion of my life. The darkness in which this apparition surrounds itself entices the night to be a moonless night, a night I discern with the tips of my fingers, with the tips of my eyelids, night I can fondle, night I can kiss like a woman, but this apparition less consistent than a dot, than smoke, slides through my fingers—the exertion to fondle it, the exertion to grasp it—surprising me in the middle of the room with a hand coiling round and throttling my throat, the oneiric precipitation of agony. The agony of a cat sauntering on the bedsheets suddenly becoming an embroidered motif. The quiet agony of a carp just before it becomes a pocketknife shaped like a carp. To gaze at a castle in ruins soon after researching its architectural plan at the municipal museum; it is impossible that you will not observe the latent agony of this woman after you have scrutinized her likeness for a very long time. After life's demoralizing agony it is to be expected that what *follows,* what I'm being appraised of, is the latent or at least the virtual agony of death.

The rattle of a poorly-closed window at the approach of the storm, the shadows cast beneath the moon by the curtains' folds, the footsteps on the roof, the delirious screen proffered by the wardrobe-mirror consulted in semi-obscurity, and all these exterior accidents capable of unleashing an entire hallucinatory network impel us to bite with flaming teeth this fruit of smoke in which grimaces, fears, amorous moments devise their trysts.

This bird whose form is not familiar to me although I know it better than I know myself, whose flight I don't understand although I breathe the air of the heights to which it hoists me, divulges its incessant presence on my shoulder through its permanent state of panic in which I find myself in each time I find myself alone. Here, there is no discussion about a trickling towards a prototypically histrionic set of kindred horrors. I am scared of the door, I am scared of the moon, I am scared of the mirror, I am scared of the curtains, but what I sense in the vicinity of this phantastic bird of night has nothing in common with infantile fear in the middle of the night vis-à-vis creaking and shadows. Bird of night, day, bird of five-in-the-morning or of the month of December, bird of red or the river, of pallor, of dagger, of travel, of hatred or love, bird of love or bird of velvet, bird of scents or bird of stone, bird of paralysis or bird of doesn't-matter-what, unnamed bird, unphotographed bird, unseen bird, bird beyond speaking, bird which you couldn't find any better way to hold in contempt except by pronouncing that it is more an idea than a bird, burning bird, freezing bird, neither freezing bird nor burning bird, *unremembered* bird, refused by memory and affirmed by desire bird, bird that broke loose on a spring morning from the cage of a dream erased from a memory and which I scaled in the way blood rises, first up to the chest, then from the chest to the tempest, from the tempest to the shoulder, with fingers from which peel away as when, after a fire, slices of burnt circles under eyeballs peel away, flesh in ruins.

I am trying to remember what is told about what passes through the brain of a hanged man: is it a scarf that I toss from one shoulder to the other in order to artificially provoke a forest wind? Is it a silk fan to perfume myself with? Is it a ladder to descend down a fountain?... All of the answers appear and are indeed possible, true. It is perhaps the bracelet that an unknown woman should offer me from the window of a train in the station. The train leaves the station, the woman smiles at me, she waves with her handkerchief, with her hair, I remain alone upon the platform, I am too filled with emotion to move, to do anything, when through the station where I am, only a few moments later, another train appears and another woman at the window offers me another bracelet. This hallucinatory duplication of fortuitousness reminds me of yet another woman whom I must encounter, this time in my chamber, an unknown woman whom I will find one evening sprawled out in my bed, bedecked in intimate attire, leafing through a book or smoking a cigarette, an unknown woman who will ask me no questions in relation to my presence or her presence at that hour in apparently unusual circumstances and who will begin speaking to me as if we were continuing an interrupted conversation. I remember down to the smallest details all that will take place and forget everything that has already taken place. What pains me is that at times I even forget what will take place. We will have to recall that in a mountain train station, in a dark tunnel, on a stairs, on a river or on a field our fingers will encounter each other, they have encountered each other. It is an exchange of fires, this exchange of fingers, of kisses, of handkerchiefs.

We throw ourselves into each other's arms as if after a long absence, we who have been absent all our lives. Together we roam through passages, run over a bridge, invent a forest. The foreign tongue that fills our mouths while our nails plunge into each other's backs, our faces flooded by tears and daisies, is spiced with the undecipherable taste of leaning forward over a chasm. I continue leaning forward, deeper over the chasm in order to experience the voluptuousness of losing all sense of dimension, all certain affirmations, all respiration, my lungs are now delicate lace in the beak of a vulture. Though we never separated we are always meeting, each meeting baffles, surprises, disorients. We sleep forgetting we are awake. We ask ourselves in our slumber: are you drowsy? We offer one another apricots with our eyelashes, we kiss our fingers with grasses, with frost. With vertiginous speed we transmute almost simultaneously from solid to liquid, from liquid to gas, from gas to hallucination. This stone is you, this fire is you, this departure is you. We suspect our presence from the shadows cast upon the earth by trees, the eclipses of the moon, the cat's nocturnal trysts. Any phenomenon, any occurrence, the most common objects become, in the light of this permanent waiting, a message. With a single flower emerging from the buttonhole, the panic, a single pull of the comb's teeth, the fainting spell. All the forgotten dreams of the last twenty years return to our lives without being scrutinized by our memory, without being fondled by our fingers. The dreams in our gloves, the dreams under our veils, incessantly present beneath their absent flesh. The tunnel I traverse between presence and absence, between past and future, is at the same time a revolving elevator in which the images impose themselves despite their absence of contour and their reality is all the more certain as we recognize through foreshadowing, through breaths of air, through the accelerated pounding of the blood flow. The pyramids are concrete examples of forgotten dreams. The Great Secret as well. Nicholas Flamel in his ambulatory delirium on the way to Spain forgets one dream. Raymond Roussel's Africa is a forgotten dream. A forgotten dream the crystal, prehistory and tomorrow's history, epilepsy, the crimes we realize without knowing whom we murdered and why and *if* we murdered indeed, the flight, especially the flight, this birdless, wingless flight, this magic word we used to know, this magic word we misplaced, this magic word we haven't encountered yet, the poems written with fire and water on paper made of wax. I myself am a wax figure, I melt on your shoulder, your body shaking with tears, with tears. The thwarted thunderbolts afflict me, the impending rains that threaten without falling, the conventional conclusion of horror novels. I amble between morning and evening, between your entrance and exit from your room, with the clumsiness of a night bird forced to imitate a chicken. I understand nothing except the nights, moonless or not, stormless or not, the nights that turn your presence into falling soot, that shift your wavering presence into a single illusion, the nights holding hands that never touch, we plunge together down a stairwell that doesn't hold us, towards the castle that the Middle Ages forgot to build. Lover with lashes eternally closed, gaze at my phosphorate eyeball, the horse bitten by nightingales, the armor greased with sunflower oil and stars. See the torture chamber of memory, see the horse stables, see the reception hall. We invite ourselves to our first castle, each time overtaken by the agitation of our first ball. Do you still know your name, do you recognize your cheeks, your customs? I open wide the door toward the chamber in the tower, the chamber with alembics and old manuscripts, with the magic circle shrouded by spiders, the furnace in ruins next to the skeleton of a woman in the arms of a man, the chamber in which I forgot for the first time. I place my lips upon the ashes of this future chamber in order for your lips to appear even more red. I collect the fossils of this event so that when I peer over your shoulder, I will stop myself from seeing your protoplasm. Standing at the window, I shake a sheet of darkness in order for night to fall faster. The violation of this forgotten chamber coincides with violating you. Our first night of love. Your fresh blood disheveled on the floor as on a saber. You cry, you laugh, you do not know how to be happy, you do not know how to be sad, you are too happy. You kiss my mouth, my shadow. You whisper my name (whose?) as if you were putting on a velvet stocking, as if you were licking leaves. You give me endless proofs in regard to being, your magnificent being of murmur and perfume. But I will never know if it all was no more than a dream, if it was at least a dream, at least a foreshadowing. Each time I kiss you I feel the skeleton of your lips. Each time I breathe I touch a fetus.

THE ECHO PAINTED RED

Stretched out in the coffin of her own body, the streets she steps on, the long hallways hung with mirrors, the forests and rivers, become at the approach of this woman the color of the horizon an immense catafalque erected in the middle of the world, at the approach of this woman in which horizontal and vertical stand face to face in a state of permanently unstable equilibrium and about which it cannot be said whether she is floating or whether she is asleep, whether she moves or whether she quivers. Next to this deathly beautiful woman, deathly beloved, deathly unreal, the world appears for the first time as it is in reality, a cemetery vaulting birth and death, vaulting death and death.

With my black teeth in her black flesh, in a room where, high as the walls, these indefinite black mirrors reflect us to endlessness, in a black room on black sheets cloaked by a black silk blanket, I sense that the blood pounding stronger and stronger in me is red for the first time. I bite deeper and deeper into this woman's shoulder and my mouth fills with dust, or perhaps only with silence. I do not find the prints left by my teeth on the flesh into which I bit so deeply, I find them in my thirsty mouth through which it seems as if someone had fled. Maybe her shoulder took a bite out of my teeth, or maybe life and death reversed destinies. I adore the sacrilegious act this amorous tryst entails, this encounter on the edge of the grave, and I gaze at the huddle of gravediggers, petrified in the middle of the alley, as I would gaze at a landscape in the spring.

Petrified: the tears on the graves and the stones on the graves, the magnificent toil across the continents, a funeral monument, this universe fixed in its imperceptible motion below which the repulsive wheeze of the earth recalls the open eyeballs of a corpse. I met my love in the graveyard and for the first time the desire to live mingles with love, for the first time the desire to live does not traumatically counter death. Nostalgia for the natal realm and prescience of decay in death tryst in this nuptial vault where the bride puts on the coffin like a nightgown and in which the exchange of embraces seems to be an ironic offer of a kilogram in exchange for an hour. This chaotic admixture of space and time inside of a single moment the dimension of eternity and universe finds me beside this woman's coffin, without bothering to ask myself if I am attending a birth or a burial, if the interior of this coffin holds a corpse or a fetus, because I know in advance that I attend at the same time a birth and a burial and the mouth towards which I sink dies and returns to life with each kiss.

Death, and especially the sword it permanently holds over our head, which stifles our most enthusiastic impulses, reducing gesture to intention and shout to whisper, casting over the cheek transfixed by pleasure a pallor foreshadowing the shroud, this danger, so close and, until further orders so inevitable, ceased to exercise upon me its annihilating pressure. Fear of death may impede me from visibly committing acts (it will not impede me when, entrusted with a revolver, I will be the ambulatory suicide or the somnambulist murderer, conduit for the trickle of spleen) but cannot prevent the blood rising in me like the sap of a plant and when I say plant to myself I am thinking of the immediate sense of the word and not the metaphoric. I cannot commit suicide every instant, I commit suicide only once. Until then the spectre of death appears to me as a cheek, familiar and intimate, I live in its vicinity without being frightened by the legend of its grin and scythe. Life of a plant growing in a graveyard, well-versed in transforming itself once, a single time only, into a young wolf running upon the graves. Life of a plant containing this embryonic wolf in its weft, in which the gesture's apparent state of passivity encounters the intention's apparent activity, apparent dawns and dusks, apparent departures and returns, apparent life that reconciles itself better with the idea of apparent death, death as an idea which I created, without resorting to consolation through distasteful ideas of the thereafter.

Between death and apparent life love appears as the sole certitude. Ever since life and death abandoned their antagonistic positions in order to exchange places, like two rooms plunged into darkness between which the door opens, I am not capable of making love except at the edge of the grave-hole, at the edge of my own grave-hole. I feel much better in knowing that I carry a corpse inside me, that the woman I love is a spectre and that our embraces are as if reflected in a mirror. I will endure without mystical histrionics or realistic lamentations the passage from a vaguely precise form to one in dissipation, from circle to star, from animal to un-animal. And I will never understand how someone can deplore, even if it may be that of a close relative, the death of a diplomat or a butcher, the passage from their senseless organic life to inorganic life should not be seen as any more than a plate that breaks. "This dust was a butcher" or "this butcher is no longer a butcher" sounds to me like a sentence lacking content, nothing is communicated to me, nothing has taken place, it is as if a word defines itself through itself, it is as if you were to say that a butcher is a butcher.

I love a butterfly, a spider, a few stones, few scallop-shells, few crystals, people, books. My preferences do not oscillate between these forms defined by unique content, the material from which they are made having each time the transparency, attraction and consequences of an apparition. Live or dead apparition, organic or inorganic, of flesh or shadow, it enters into the constellation of my being like a nebulous beloved; this frail but certain reality, undiscernable and fascinating, fills up the time I am allotted in this landscape, an impossible feat if I were forced to accept as real the existence of the butcher, a family, a rooster, a Bible.

This reality I wend in a fog accustoms me to the idea of my decomposition in an even denser fog. I say "accustoms me" in the improper sense, in which you would say that the curtain becomes accustomed to the shadow. What I sense, however, as a direct consequence of this double game with destiny, is the terrible simulacrum of my amorous tendency toward necrophilia. I push the woman away in order to love her phantom. My masturbatory nights when I make love with the shadows of many women simultaneously. And this woman of flesh in whom I refuse to see anything other than skeleton. The cemeteries I exhume with each kiss, my accelerated breathing when I slash the belly of this woman which I am in reality caressing and the coolness of the burial vault I feel around me despite the heat of embrace and the sultriness of the summer night. The lover's mouth seems even more voluptuous when I succeed in smearing the red on the lips upon her entire face, her face now smeared with blood fills my mouth with sores, with nocturnal, undomesticated vistas. The most insignificant noise, a piece of straining furniture creaking in the middle of the night and even the bedsprings that accompany our customary embraces affright me with the thought that someone would surprise me by lifting the lid of the coffin. I doubt the reality of the woman next to me more than her absence. In her absence I never cease to see her alive even when she's a shadow, I grope her flesh, I touch her hair. At my side this woman acquires an imprecise contour and each time she moves I fear she will dissipate on the ground in a heap of dust. I don't understand the sexual act in which the partners execute simultaneously a series of opposite motions. The woman must lie underneath me with ice-cold and lightning nerves, in a position of immobility approaching a corpse's rigor in order for me to perform upon her corpse this act of active necrophilia, active to a measure of tension equaling fire, to be followed by my assumption of the passive necrophilic role in which I take the place of her perfect immobility, her place of the wounded flower.

I never forget to conceal in the most obscure corner of the room the knife and scissors; from these memory clutches sheen, velvet and depth, and I introduce as if dreaming their sharp edge into that dream abdomen which opens up to me. The woman I adore as if I were dreaming, as if I were dying, as if I weren't born yet, offers me her sublime cadaver in the ruins of this cemetery in which the night watchman in the distance, rifle sight against his eye, confuses me with a hyena.

I LOVE YOU

The objects suavely heteroclite, the button, the veins, a mustache, a guitar, a thunderbolt, the piano thrown from the window, a hat from which a very beautiful woman consumes spaghetti, a few fingers, a tie-pin, a sofa upon which rots a bed, a curtain under the moon, a bitten apricot, laundry soap next to a piece of jewelry, a spider next to a fork, and the mythology of orgy take on a voluptuously fresh significance, the rendezvous of objects borrowing the velvety feel of nebulousness and the catastrophic nature of a rendezvous of planets are flames that rendezvous with water, are voices that rendezvous their echo, amorous encounters in which paralysis is a character trait and contraction is a ferocious way of life, peaceful, mineral, I attend to this monstrous pairing of objects with the sentiment that I participate as spectator-actor to the trysts between desire and pleasure in a world of dream and of vice, I inspire the eroticism of these metallic embraces, I listen to the passionate howls the atoms communicate to me, I plunge my teeth into wood till I draw blood, into stone, paper, rags, I myself a rag among these objects of flesh in which I throttle my tears, more allusive than real, impersonal, ideal, look, this categorical knife trickling with my unsteady blood, look, my living suit of velvet clothing beneath which palpitates a spectre, an apparition, I amble among these objects fully erect, filled with inevitablity, I hear their respiration accelerated by their voluptuousness, their blood reddened by spasm as if by crime, look, this plush pile chair taking a bite out of the artificial tulip, slurping its lips and its tongue, writhing on this carpet of hair that emanates steam, the comb taking a bite from the mirror, the mirror kissing the teeth of the smile of a celluloid puppet presented by the powder case, majuscule orgy on the margin of love, at the border of dreams, at the periphery of fainting, hallucinatory pairing of possibilities and phenomena, of desires in a permanent state of accessibility, in which tensions do not disappear along with their realization, tensions become taller than flames after each satisfaction of pleasure, a state of suspense, clench and howl, the silent howl of objects trysting with their wooden veins, or glass veins ready to burst, with their teeth of frost and grass ready to burst, the bed where the tryst is consumed, being now the dimension of the universe, or of my room, the bishop in chess is no longer a clerical figure, he is enamored of his queen with his hand upon his chest, with the rose between the teeth of the beloved, the beloved's teeth being now a rain shower of stars in his black, disheveled hair, hair through which the wind blows like walls collapsing to ruin, like blooming willows, love liberated from human fetters now sings unrestrained on a scale invented by delirious desires, desires vitreous and cold like lightning, on the surface of the world or of my room, love liberated from the human, this compromise, intrudes through the most sweltering door into the inside of the stewed objects, these brides, disheveled objects, carnivore, sanguine, the magic objects that surround me and divulge their secrets one by one, these women with endless numbers of genders in which mystery wears a mask of petrified cruelty, of virtual avalanche in which the snow is made of void, an automatic mask, an automatic chair, an automatic flower scattering an automatic scent in an automatic room, Heron of Alexandria, Bacon, Van Helmont, and all other genial builders of automata that I think about each time I stare at the outside of an object as if from inside, each time I stare at a door, a mirrored wardrobe, a tie-pin, a wax doll, I automatize them in an automatic mode, they acquire their own life (which the fabulistic cretinism of an Aesop or La Fontaine has attempted to compromise with didacticism), a unique individuality, a hallucinatory and mechanic amble which completes my travels and fright, which fills my dreams and vigils with a world of clatter, of colors, of disheveled veils and coiffures, tenebrous and sublime golems discovered inside the most common objects, the most indifferent, I touch a fork and unleash an entire network of possibilities, a very complicated apparatus is put into motion as if the fork were a factory of questions, of impulses and spectres, a door opens inside it leading toward a hallway at the end of which a mirror reflects me upside-down in my medieval costume, another door leads toward the childhood's phosphorous room where the sleeping princess has been awaiting me for one hundred years in order never to wake again, another door leads toward a window or the bottom of a fountain, this fork which I put to sleep with my magnetic gaze, my vitreous eyeball, crosses the room with a somnambulistic step, touches the doorbells and the walls, kisses me on the forehead with her protracted rhinoceros teeth, traverses me, dreams me, the fork, the moon, or a glass of water, these inoffensive objects exploding in my hand like a button that a child plays with till he swallows it, they rendezvous, they sniff each other, breathe each other, salute each other and murder each other reciprocally with a hunting rifle, they separate, bearing in the heart, bleeding, a bayonet or nightingale, around the first corner the glass of the fumigating streetlamp will caress the antelope skin of a wrinkle sprouting on the forehead of this fourteen-year-old girl or will make love with the leaves, the glass of the streetlamp may become an infernal machine in my hand if instead of sprinkling it like a garden I put it on my lips next to the lightning, the automata pass

me or through me, I rub them with my arms or my tissues, I
hide behind the door so the table won't see me, I hide under-
neath the table so the pocketknife won't look for me, this ten-
der game between no and no is attended also by the forest and
the four birds of prey out of which the most ferocious is soli-
tude, is attended also by my pearl necklace, black gloves, the
pallor and the echo, the voluptuous clitoris of this echo that
illuminates my room like a lamp and like an agony, a silver tray
falling from the cupboard and onto the floor, from the floor
directly into the void as if it never existed, as if nothing ever
happened, it reminds me of the witch who cast a spell over me,
curing me of epilepsy with two broom strands and a few grams
of lead, instead of falling to the floor the ashes of the cigarette
I am smoking in the darkness rise up, they are a vibrant tree
upon whose branches a songbird of ashes sings, out of her
voice break apart large pieces of asphalt like an excavated city,
with a magnifying glass under my eyes I follow the virus of
this voice, its motions of melted beast, its throbbing on the
palpitating and undecided margin of the real, its transmuta-
tion back into flame, the virus of this flame, soil shifts inside
a match, the terminated dirt of this compass, the strictly for-
bidden entrance of that denture, the back-door exit of the win-
dow or the service door entrance of the stones, look, all the
possibilities of doing exactly the opposite of everything that
imposes itself upon us and just as much color that the fragility
of a wolf pack stalking a sled lends to our walk, look, this piece
of domesticated dynamite for my personal use while my tie
becomes a hanging rope, without any scruples I would launch
the axiom that two mirrors placed before each other reflect a
third, a fourth, a fifth, I wash myself in mirrors, I go to sleep
in mirrors, all objects surrounding me are mirrors, they reflect
each other and reflect me, my bones are inside them, my
nerves are at the window instead of a flag, my ear is glued to

the floor in order for me to listen to the horse-hoof clatter of the bricks, perhaps I haven't left home yet, perhaps I haven't left my childhood yet, perhaps I am galloping across a field on my wooden horse, nostrils scattered by sabers crossing in the wind, lips unraveled by feverish murmurs, teeth narcissistically thrust into my own tongue while in my bed disheveled by passions comb and hair pair up scandalously like two snakes.

BLOOD AND MEMORY'S DÉCOLLETAGE

The dagger, the stabs to my heart I sustain in the darkness with studied violence, with an adorable precision, with a sense of aggression developed to the point of jackal, the jackal criss-crossed by the fossils of agony, of foreshadowing, of artificial breathing, the fossils of the sewing machine stitching a fabric of dust or a cloth of willows for the costume of stars worn by somnambulists, compel me to savor the unease of being a pre-destined victim, frightened and ridiculous rabbit before this beloved who fossilically stalks me, mutating with unrivaled ease her superb and obsidian marble-like neck from lace choker to a collar of vipers. I like to weep with tears of flowers on my own shoulder, now an icy forehead beneath which a bell rings. Each tear reminds me of the morbid necessity inherent to certain aquatic creatures, of coming up to the surface of the water and abandoning with aplomb their own respiratory system, thus making their entrance into death, like certain phantoms make an entrance into life. I position myself between these two possibilities of toppling the real and, at their point of rendezvous, the flame I wear on my heart like a kiss reminds me of the woman with icy forehead beneath which a bell rings, who plants her lips on my heart's lips, an embrace performed at the risk of our own combustion. With chest on fire, with swollen veins uncoiled over my jacket like ropes, eyes bulging with violet ash, I consume my desperation, sublime and lovely, uncompromised by vague expectations or prospects, a total desperation approaching a total absence of hope.

During these instants of sadistic recess, when my arms preserve a martyr's immobility, when my claws, that I took such pains to sharpen, swarm about my fingers, inoffensive butterflies, when fury itself, which never abandons me, is an attenuated smoke, warm and anesthetic, I think about the dalliance of the viper and the spider, and for the first time I do not envy these horrendous representatives of human passion, I envy the blood that flows for the last time in their victims. I am the victim of those eyes that fascinate me in the darkness and I don't know what exactly inebriates me the most, the disquiet that they nurture with so much diabolical skill or the stab of the dagger that she will crown my head with, splintering it as you would an apple in order to take a bite out of the worm. I would weep tears of rocks and bats if my abiding sadism weren't traversed from time to time by these morbidly passive inclinations, if the necessity to murder, to spit, to insult and to eat the object of dalliance were not interrupted by the pleasure of being murdered by my own victim. I can't tolerate for more than five minutes this masochistic inebriation but if these five minutes were absent from my life I am certain that my life, the vitreous tint of blood, would become livid and herbivorous like rictus' disfiguring grin. Even Satan, that exemplar, allowed himself to be insulted by God, that whale. I would like him to divulge to me during one of the nights when he sustains me with his nocturnal angel's conversation, just how clandestine was the pleasure of that singular moment so full of consequences. Frightened by her own audacity, my beloved awakens beside me displaying an impudence that she herself will not recognize, she stares at her bloody fingers, the wound she sees on my chest startles her, I can't tell whether her hallucinatory eyes are asking for punishment or forgiveness, I can't tell whether her real or simulated horror is a provocation, a stimulant, a powerful aphrodisiac for my future journeys into her sublime being. On my livid cheeks the tears haven't dried yet, I haven't yet finished savoring this moment, in which the upheavals of perspective, of morals, of blood have satisfied the most demanding expectations, when between my shoulders I feel the plunge of the second dagger, this time luminous, volcanic, savage, the dagger on whose razor-sharp blade I read the entirety of my yet unsatisfied hatred, the entirety of my ancestral fury, all those forests in flames swarming our internal nights, and my being partakes in this abrupt passage from virginal to bestial state as a medusa kisses a tree, introducing its tongue into its hollows and its teeth into lightning, disheveling stage entrances and exits like the hair of a wild boar caught in a splinter, the impatient skidding from one discontent to another, from one instrument of torture to another, with the feeling that every act is a guillotine to which you submit the head of the first question you are asked, the answers you give yourself afterward assume other instruments of torture, for instance a horse far larger than in reality into whose belly slides a kilogram of dynamite you mixed with its hay, a spurious horseman riding this horse beyond measure, intangible, visible and invisible behind the horizon from which you mark its gallop, with two pistols in each hand, with a flock of birds in each pistol, with the beloved's white neck between your teeth instead of the bit, familiar oneiric journey, how fervent I become as I behold in you the cruelty of each atom contouring my being when with one temple resting on a dead man, the other on a living one I oscillate between two cliffs as between the humps of a single camel.

I became drowsy from so much sleep, I am finally ready to sleep, I sleep in restaurants while I eat, I sleep while I bathe and I sleep while I look in the mirror. One night a woman I didn't love, while looking for a libidinous diminutive for my name, called me somnambulist. Why didn't I love this woman who spoke so appealingly; why do I love the one who gave me a horrible name? Why do the women we love and whom we never miss a chance to abuse sometimes surpass themselves in abusing us? Why do I enjoy asking myself exactly the same questions that my baker asks himself? The histrionic entrance of this text, all the anxiety it leaks, and even the anguish that tints each of its sentences with the eyeball of an owl and a gash may be summarized in the final analysis to this last banal question, which I ask myself no differently than the baker. If writing cannot lead to a final analysis, to what we have chosen to call final analysis, then I forsake writing with greater ease than I forsake hunting. I reject a rendezvous with my own caricature on these roads of ruin, in the underbelly of these abandoned mines where I like to saunter surrounded by my slender hounds, their brows wounded by a lance. I prefer to abandon my text where reality begins to threaten it, to intimidate it, and obliterating the last sentence with the crimson lead of my pencil, I turn over in order to go back to sleep. Why do I immediately begin dreaming of an anonymous woman reading to me a breathtaking page from her breathtaking life, listening to her with death-like gravity, in a state of panic-stricken admiration without bounds, tears flowing unawares from my eyeballs and onto my chest rent in grief. So that after a few moments, this exceptional woman will offer the most imbecilic observation that I ever heard, a veritable observation-douche: not even Heine, a truly cultured man, ever wept so much. What happened? Who wakes me from my dream without actually waking me? Who disturbs the dream's magnificent sense of the absurd with the mediocrity of external logic? The fainting spell, this scarf that flutters on my lips and flavors my breath with the magnetism of a kiss, a kiss upon her hair, a kiss upon her calves, guides my steps at times in the direction of those borderline terrains, one foot in a crystal estate, the other proceeding towards mire. Last night I fainted on the terrace of a lady friend and listened once again to such a peripheral conversation: each star is a sun, I am perturbed by the existence of comets, if we survey the earth from the reference point of anything we see in the sky, our insignificant size, etc. Their interior language, anxious, tortured, terrified by the grandiose celestial phenomena in which they unconsciously participate, proceeded to mix imperceptibly with the language of the first popular astronomy manual, and we all woke up in a realm more demoralizing than the high-school principal's office, in a realm where the only possible reaction is our howl of laughter lasting an entire century. When it finally became quiet, I went to sleep again. The man and the woman continued their conversation. I don't know what they were talking about, I do know however that they were telling each other exactly the opposite of what they wanted to tell each other, not one of us knew what exactly we wanted to tell each other, not even I who was asleep. It got cold, the woman left in order to change, I said something to the man, about food, he laughed, I went back to sleep, the woman now wore a jacket and a pair of white pants, she wore a knee on her chest, it choked her, she was stunningly beautiful even when I looked at her with open eyes. I am sure that I need to communicate to them some very important things that I will never learn about, that they too need to communicate to me something that the rest of my life possibly depends upon, I can read this in the furtive looks we exchange, the direct ones too, a little frightened by the shifting sands of these eyeballs, deliriously propped up by their internal crutches, the utter lack of knowledge of these crutches, proceeding forward in the dark with outstretched hands each time we kiss or reject each other, let's meet tomorrow at four, I am tired, I bought blue fabric for a dress, I love you, I loathe, it demoralizes me, the tendency of passive women of perpetrating from time to time their sadism upon me, I will renounce this metal eyeball and replace it with a phosphorous one, don't kill me, please don't kill me, if you knock on the door I am sure no one will open it, doors are made to be wrenched out of their jambs, the woman: I am waiting for a man who will torture me with wet sheets, the first man: I won at cards last night, I am offering you money, the second man: I will take the money even though you humiliate me (joke? pederasty? persecution? bravado?) the woman: I am going to prepare dinner, the first man: is she insane? the second: I don't love her, the first: I find you at times unspeakably ugly, the second: you have to be even uglier for me to love you, the woman: my mother is a horrible human being, vulgar, the first man: I think she's more beautiful than a queen... What happened, what is going to happen, what is contained in this inspired fluid that traverses through my hair without touching my skull. I don't love this woman, I love this man, I love another woman, that woman demoralized me, I don't love that woman, you can hear the fireman from the station across the way taking off to put out a fire, a star fell, what are falling stars, why do we meet every evening, why do we see each other, why do I wish to see no one, I will bring you a lamp, I would like a straw hat, there are certain people who etc., come tomorrow, looks like a steamship, my heart pounds, I need a glass of water, can you tell the future in coffee grounds? please don't kill me, turn on and turn off the light, your shirt is wet, I burned my finger, wake him up because I am tired, I am going back to sleep, I sleep deeply for twelve hours, I wake up in the morning so I can go back to sleep another twelve hours, today I am not going to the beach, a few nights from now we'll have full moon again, I have never been so alone, I will always be so alone, I tear the petals of this field flower and have the feeling I tear out my fingers, the fingers of my hand or the fingers of my glove, the fingers of my love? the fingers in the hollow of the palm or those in the wrinkles of my forehead? open a box in which I hid a photograph and find the leper of this photograph, I loathe counting to ten, I will count to nine, this deceitful and diabolical number I adore like a fetish, that I adore like a goodbye I am going to grits myself, like an I will never write again a sentence before I convince myself of its utter separation from memory. The traps the preconscious sets for me, I will use them to trap mice. Goodbye. Whoever digs a hole for another falls all by himself, give everyone my regards, today is a wonderful day and other proverbs that grin at me from the mirror with an impertinent candor.

THE RUBBER COFFEE

The sumptuous mantles of blood which certain prairie vistas toss upon their shoulders just before the moment of the storm, the ravenous lynx's eyeball the horizon hones upon us when it surprises us alone in the middle of the field, the roots of the trees, these trees turned upside-down in which the worms are birds in the same way that the image on the retina turns upside-down those on the outside, the volcanoes, especially the volcanoes, before which our limited virility acquires enormous proportions infused by desire, if our desires boasted a sex in accord with the volcanoes certainly our lovemaking would take place through volcanoes, we would fill women with lava and the fruit of this languorous coupling would not be culled from the traumatic vaginal birth, we would unearth it a thousand years later under the ruins of our own combustion like archeologists who unearth themselves, erotic births and deaths, passionate separations and reunions, with the reassuring presence of this volcano in full erection and this scenic mother who is delighted to suffer our sadism, and then there are the forests and the oceans, the nocturnal forests in which we enjoy getting lost, getting scared, it appears that with each tree struck by lightning a part of our old, histrionic anxieties dissipate as well, while the furious oceans restore the incipient connection between water and fire, an ocean of flames and a forest of water, lightning oscillating between one and the other with the same velocity that a waterfall becomes electricity and then there are the legendary roc birds, the elegant bats, the carnivorous plants with their untouchable teeth, with their unhurried bites as if blowing into a lantern, the sharks, the butterflies, these crystallizations that learned to fly, this snow, certain flowers such as for instance the tuberose and the calla lily, the plants from which morphine, opium and hashish are extracted, the misleading stars, lyrical, astrological, fixed and falling, veiled, their thin lips reflecting the gleaming dagger, their fascinating respiration, inhuman universe, un-zoological, vitreous, displaying a pallor recalling that of the first assassin and the first victim, the stars, rain of stars, snow of stars, sun of stars and shadow of stars, nebulae, grottoes, a comet, vampires, certain crustaceans, a few rocks, look, so many magnificent signs we find like a lost diamond in an ocean of mire, so many revealing signals inciting us to spy a parallel universe that mirrors them, that mirrors us, these isolated elements of nature negate nature, denounce it, violate it, they introduce un-nature into nature in the same way that we introduce the unnatural into people's natural lives, this comet, these vampires, these storming forests are us, us and our friends from the lunatic asylums and the barricades, for a few thousand years now I can't prevent myself from vomiting when faced with this nauseating spectacle that nature offers us, nature after the taste of the Creator, resembling as two drops of urine do the taste of the first greengrocer, nature with flowers, grass, sunsets and sunrises, look, the landscape enchanting the celestial eye of this scowling and senile old man who, during Sunday's rest ambulates his creature through his pre-paradisiacal garden. All this constipating green, a veritable diarrhea of nature, all these melancholy trees by the side of the road, the water that flows quietly like a buffalo masticating grass, this philosophical grass, this horizon compromised by sunsets and sunrises, and even beyond the horizon, this disgustingly scenic planet, disgustingly natural, disgustingly descriptive, provokes the urgent desire to vomit, to spit, to excrete as after a sinister enema performed upon us by the Creator himself. I hate too much the idea of paradise for its earthly parody not to infuriate me. But beyond these samples of vegetal bon-bons, beyond these moral landscapes, beautiful, good, healthy, I spy even now their infernal negation, inside the volcanoes in full eruption, in the embraces of earthquakes, in the sultry kisses of floods, inside a shell the sea throws at me from a distance, in the destiny that the stars pronounced to me, in this precipice I like to plunge in from the highest peak of the mountain, gliding like a bird of prey, outstretched arms, the journey ending adolescently in pollution, no one in this landscape wonders that a phenomenon fated to end in mortal agony culminates in amorous convulsions, in the amorous and amoral landscape where the vegetal and the mineral suffer the frantic consistency of our blood. I emerge from between the lips of these carnivorous plants or from the kidney of this crystal and burst directly into Africa. I am disgusted by natural Africa in which civilized humanity introduces its weapons and its missionaries, I am not afflicted with a weakness for exoticism, and besides equatorial heat does not agree with me. On the other hand, I visited Raymond Roussel's Africa. Our internal geography does not correspond to nature. The region I roam is planted with hair, short and soft, the first virginal ornament my groundskeeper procured for me, shearing all the girls under the age of twelve over an expanse stretching for many kilometers. I walk as if I were their hymen which was planted there, as if I kissed a leaf and if I close my eyes I see within a room of drawn curtains all of these girls, one hand on their hairless sex, scalded by sultry, desolate tears. I don't know why my hand grips an open umbrella, but while I am walking, holding it tight in my hand in order for it not to take to the air, I take a bite from a live bird, a pigeon I think. I eat for a long time and don't understand why I can't get past the feathers of this bird, why I cannot get to the flesh. I stretch myself upon the ground without letting go of the umbrella in my hand nor interrupting for one moment my extenuated lunch. In the meanwhile, the hair that I lie upon is grown, is now boundless blue coiffure. I try to caress it with my free hand, I brush it with my fingers, I scratch it, am overtaken by the irresistible need to kiss it, in fact it is what I do although my mouth is full of pigeon and feather down. I see a twelve-year-old girl running over the field as if trying to escape from me. I tell myself it must be "the idea of possessing a twelve-year-old girl" and I get up in order to chase her. I am pushing a baby carriage on water. I have the sensation that I have found a new swimming style and think about showing it the following day to a woman at the beach; pushing a baby carriage replaces the movement of the arms and legs. The child inside wails and whimpers and I have the feeling that he swims much faster when he is crying. I am swimming faster and faster. I am in the baby carriage in the place of the child and I recall a picture I saw a few years before representing a tree in a boat. The baby carriage hurtles down a sloping street and I'm afraid we'll crash into a wall and shatter.

Undomesticated regions, virgin, demented, that I traverse with the certainty of an infernal explorer, the street on which I live is far more unfamiliar, the stairs I climb daily to get to my room inspire me with less confidence than this unequalled prairie which I roam, drunk like a river. From one landscape to the next, from one collision of ruins to the next the universe regenerates itself each moment aiding the nascence of the world without simultaneously aiding the useless intellectual bloodshed that has occurred each time man attempted to pound his forehead against the cause of the cause, against the antecedence of the chicken or the egg, I roam the landscapes of my dreams and my dreams do not acknowledge the existence of naturalist landscapes. I infiltrate the landscape with horizons infinitely multiplying those that Yves Tanguy unfolds before me, I drop by the world of Max Ernst's mineral flora, I return to the devastated infantile realms which Paalen awakens in my memory, with the feeling that I roam from one dream to the next, from a continent of questions to a universe of answers. Before nature however, in the way it offers itself to me, shamelessly, each time nausea for humanity leads my steps toward the edges of the city, out of the city, there, where the prairie begins, the hill, the mountain, the lake, the oaks, I feel as much the stranger, I feel as brutalized and wounded as I do among humans.

I have never been a more vehement partisan, more devoted and rabid, of crimes against nature than I am now.

A FEW AGRICULTURAL DEVICES

It is only the cankerous frog pasted to my face that lends my appearance a misleading and lugubrious quality when, during my evening walks alongside walls, people have the impression that it is a piece of wall that moves alongside them, a kilogram counterweight of iron or stone, this mask that creeps into my wrinkles and underneath my eyelids like a dirty rag mantling my cheeks, a tear mixed with urine, as if it were the bars of a circus cage separating beasts from humans, I myself unable to decide which is the captive side and content with the vague sensation that I am visiting an immense zoological garden stocked with humans in which I am the single spectator and if I didn't experience the opposing sensation that I am the one who is looked at from the outside like a captive beast, if I didn't feel the sadness inspired by the understandable quantitative difference between myself and them, the preconception of number and majority, the fact I am alone would be nothing but the tooth of that prehistoric animal discovered by Couvier, which, although only a tooth, is more real and alive than the entire vanished species which it attempts to suggest, I would like to be the putrid tooth of my species, the black and atrophied organ out of which no power is able to reconstitute this human with his appendix, his mustache, his shoes, this human which I can't hope to convey except in the manner in which a photograph of the bride is an account of a deflowering, in the manner in which the blood in the test tube presupposes the details, the causes and the heroes of a crime, in the same manner that my eyeballs burning in their sockets and my lips cold as despair remind, describe and summarize this head of felt, this head, round like tenderness, this head humans bolster upon their shoulders without fear, without shame, as if it went without saying that you wear your excrement atop your neck, this exhibitionism of pestilence and odium, of human stupidity and exhaustion, which only a dirt-filled trunk buried for the duration of a few thousand centuries might be able to reconstitute in a museum of the future but in no case my forehead, my hair, my blood wandering mindlessly within the arteries like a ravenous wolf, my cranium shattered against the wall, my melancholy suffocated as from a knee pushed against the chest, the fingers you caress with, you claw with, the fingers I bite and kiss with, this tenebrous eyeball that I hone upon my lover from a distance like the magnetism between stars, the immense, infinite, convulsive amorous substance that fills my bones with a marrow of perfume, how can this bone, more dazzling than fury, assist in the prehistoric reconstitution of this streetcar ticket-taker with his head plunged into his cap or that banker with his kidneys more jelly than milk. This bartender with his apron, this intellectual with problems, this proletarian with a tractor, this peasant with earth, this porter with arms, this vagabond with lice, this industrialist with family, this sailor with ship may in the best case scenario represent my digestive apparatus at a given moment, that is during the era when my stomach carried a useless and protracted battle with my lungs, an excremental era, religious and social. I can reproduce if you wish my contact with my school, my prison, my landlord, with all these unfriendly pieces of furniture that I sit on, with all those horrific houses that I live in, they can even reproduce the Hardmuth No. 2 pencil that I write with or my Zentka watch that I stare at in a relative hurry in order for me not to vomit at each contact I make with the oppression of beings and things.

Only a hallucinated cup or a watermelon would be deluded enough to think that there are common traits between myself and humans, in the same way that to a European all blacks look the same, in the same way that when the calendar reads April 23rd all those named George receive congratulations despite the astrological laws that separate them.

Only a deluded eyeball, a rational eyeball can confuse this character spewed from the volcano together with lava, separated from the rocks together with dust, emerging from the maternal womb not with a vague longing to return but with a uterine reality so concrete that it appears to have never exited, only the cursory bookkeeping of this deluded eyeball might take me for a man of the office or man of the field, man of the factory or man of literature, man who incorporates the idea of atonement and sin into his most rudimentary gestures. But not only does my appearance on earth have nothing in common with the genesis of all other humans (these humans who have taken the idea of sin to the point of scabrous necessity in inventing an ideal character born of a virgin) but the predominating phenomena of life and death themselves and even this phenomenon that seems to incorporate everyone and everything, love, death and love of which it is said that everyone must pass through as if passing through a *camera oscura* built inside us, as if passing through a dagger of fate, not even here, especially here my blood circulates at a distance of several solar systems away from all other humans. Love, love that has long ceased to be for me the red thread, circulates through me, love which is now for me a vast weft, complicated and ferocious, enveloping my bones, my eyelids, my voice and each instant, which fills me and which I fill, this content and container of my life from which the demons have made for themselves a mantle of flames, from which the stars have borrowed their dazzle, mystery, grandeur, obscurity, unending love, concrete love, concrete like fingernails and hair color, like the shadow I throw upon the earth under the moon, like the window, what afflicted mind, what revolting and ironic brain can bring it near this occasional preoccupation, partial, amputated, episodic, superficial, spermatozoidal and sentimental which defines love between man and woman as being inherent to the human species? This man unhinged by adolescence breaks out of his boarding school in the middle of the night, out of his barracks, his factory job, his parental home and creeps like a plunderer in search of women. If he is not frightened enough by the strange world he enters, by the distance separating the world he leaves behind for an hour from the one he aims to gain, more in order to visit than to discover, then he starts to jeer and taunt, turns vulgar, insolent, bullish, cynical. This male who resolves his spermatozoidal conflict as if he were getting a vaccine, will resolve in the same manner his sentimental conflict, with a woman whom he will allow himself to love only when he calculates himself mature enough and serious enough for such a feat, that is exactly at the point when he is no longer capable of loving, the union of man and woman being for him an escape from love, a cure for love. Men whose only preoccupation is to grow grain and manipulate machines, these men are right when they run away from love, when they get married or cohabitate all they do is murder love, to remove it like a cyst. Their lamentable, nauseating sentimental effluvia, their I-love-yous, their I-work-only-for-yous, and even when their heart pounds, what a hideous spectacle! But their nuptial bed, what sinister worms entwine under the sheets when they throw at each other a few oppressingly hygienic grams, when they reciprocally perpetuate and nurture their false impotencies and frigidities, what philanthropic organizations circulate through their wet blood, what pestilential canals trickle through rushed embraces, their honest and obligatory embraces.

If what humans call love is the encounter of two imbecile hearts, two rudimentary genders, if what they deem love is the mutual melting of two depletions into a single being (or a third being), of two brutalizations, of two turmoils, two emotional palpitations, two excrements, if they can call life the existence on earth of a policeman, of a peasant and of an Arthur Rimbaud, if they can call death the earthly departure of a restorer and of Robespierre, as far as I am concerned, let me open the dictionary at random and say horse instead of their kind of love, fork instead of their death, burnt sugar instead of their freedom, potato peeler instead of their embraces, thresher or sphere or trigonometry instead of anything that concerns them and doesn't concern me and if the human who spends twelve hours or one hour before a machine, preoccupied by existence as by a curse is capable of love, then I would say that God does exist, that good and beautiful do exist, that the man with a purse who crosses the street in a hurry is a real character, that this coffin is real and the corpse inside and the people with tears on their faces and the flowers and the gravedigger with his general's headgear and the pedestrians who respectfully salute are real, real and necessary and fatal then too, sin, work, slavery, the hat, produce and delicatessen, vestibule and living room, prisons, cemeteries.

Fortunately, I do not acknowledge the love, the life, the death or even the birth of humans, and if my megalomania is not sufficient enough for me to claim that these disturbing phenomena are relevant only to me, I acknowledge only a few of the enamored lovers, a few spectres, these lines of fire, dazzling and magnificent, belonging to existence, pass through them as through a constellation of hearts. In the same way that I will never seek a god in a constellation of stars, I will never seek man in these constellations of hearts, man on earth and gods in heavens, these images of nothingness reflected in a prison's mirror, these images of hemorrhoid veins and piracy.

And only rationalism, the same rationalism that provided the human brain with the mustache of logic and bookkeeping, the same rationalism that raised upon his cranium a marble altar toward which paralysis strides on a horse while premises and conclusions swarm around him like so many shoes or the bust of Beethoven raised to the rank of equestrian statue, only this rationalism which fills the head of this man from one temple to the other can see in the author of these lines a case of acute misanthropy, the idea of misanthropy fully satisfying his senile dash from premise to conclusion. This Alexander the Great of contemporary society would love to stuff me in a barrel next to Diogenes in order to admire me in peace, he would love for me to tell him that the lamp I grasp between my fingers in order to darken the darkness is nothing but a lamp I use to search for a man or at the worst to set Rome on fire.

Between misanthropy and philanthropy, human stupidity devours the relationships between humans without any awareness of the inhuman relationships that I have been maintaining during the last few years with this species in ruins, vis-à-vis which the idea of misanthropy and philanthropy seems to me more abstract and chaotic than that of any hat, my relationships with humans being closer to those established by a wolf chasing a sled down the road, his hunger for blood excluding the misanthropic, the philanthropic and the hat.

From the bottom of the darkness in which I move like a somnambulist and like a wolf, I spy from a distance the species of man with its hideous thorax and encased in a carapace.

THE NEXT DAY

The vitreous thigh of suicide has begun to stalk me. Like so many daggers it flings into my face her aromatic tattoos, her scars of spices and vertigo, the wagons of burnt kidneys of this aphrodisiacal season toward which my brains slowly glide as if on a sloping highway where young women with bare breasts bite the lips of older women, these older women: your mothers and grandmothers violated out of their desire to create scandal on the streets more than their desire for pleasure, during the entire sexual act they keep upon their heads the outmoded and frigid hat like two pianos sucked by a vampire while passionately clutching beneath their arm infested with spiders all our school awards, the paralyzing mothers, devouring, castrating, mothers I point to from a distance with my finger while my leg sinks down to the knee into the mire of this room without teeth, without hair, without bed, without windows, from a window which is more imagined than external I denounce my mother, the animated multitudes are marching towards the street smelling of milk and school, the streets that elderly women sprayed with their vitriolic blood, their blood violated with the pocketknife or with the saw, their blind-woman blood regaining its sight, their blood knocked over by a car.

Why is it that suddenly my cranium, affixed to my shoulders with special care, rattles thoughtlessly at the approach of the storm or the guillotine? I lean my back against this wall that materialized like a miracle next to my weariness and my back fills up with bricks like a leper. My fingers feverishly unlock the door, the doorknob I clench burns my fingers and expels the crows from my phalanges like pigeons from a house on fire. My phalanges of ash are so many gigantic eggs swarming with crime. Crime may be a pigeon, like a rhyme. Crime and the crow make love on my fingerprints and their tender pairing gives birth to imprudence, simulacra, despair. The pairing of imprudence and simulacra makes my fingernails grow while my hair fills up with devastated forests like an inebriated child crossing the street. Only number one makes me flustered now, only number six endows my foot with the dimensions and destiny of a motorboat while numbers eight and eleven, calmer and more velvety, go to sleep upon my shoulders in imitation of cats. The horses inside the cats are shod with horseshoes too minute for the sun to rise, horseshoes created from spider lips, withered flowers, from despair without cause. From this despair without cause grows all the openings of shoe stores, the salesmen in a state of immobility, like people on death row. Proceeding from the window displays a few women march forward toward the interior of the store on a carpet of smoke, their knees illuminated from within with a diamond, their veins illuminated from within with a reflector, their suction-skirts drawing darkness between their thighs like so many oil fields, while their thighs, ventilated by a skin of fans, march forward like wind toward the shoes. The shoes then develop magnetic properties, erotic, they murder the women with a stiletto issuing from the sole or from what could be named: the ferocious revenge of unfathomable objects. The store owner will appear too late in his limestone frock coat, he telephones his wife to say he will be late for dinner and places his lips on the first shoe with the sensation of touching a battery cell. The vista opens suddenly in the shoe like a door: if you lock the door with your ear instead of sniffing it as some do, the vista develops a few nervous tics such as: the vertiginous gait of mountains from nose to eyeball and back, the transport of poplars into closed rooms, the cementing of flowing waters with the aid of photography, the systematic cultivation and maintenance of volcanoes, etc. Towards these devouring vistas, about which anything can be said, even that they are odious or too flaccid, except in any case that they do not exist, the city sometimes advances, in the evening, when it lies the bed down upon its weariness rather than the other way around, when pieces of asphalt peel off the skin of men and women, eclipsing the onion. The onion of windmills found in the vertigo of men and women, positioned two meters away from the morbid necessity of certain plants to mechanize themselves, join forces in order to impart the dastardly cowardice of the horizon. The horizon, only when it is a jockeycap on the forehead of a philosopher, only when it bites the leg of the suffocating propensity of stones to metamorphose into birds, steps away from itself by a few centimeters. It then encounters the pedestal upon which it ascends, youthful and proud, in order to regard itself in perspective like a black and white sketch. An escalator binds the pedestal and stones together, while the horizon, arm in arm with the ocean, traverses the long, obscure chambers in which each minute thousands of somnambulists breathe their last. Memory's somnambulists, disintegration's somnambulists blow kisses to the somnambulists of hypnotism lessons and exchange among themselves scarves, top hats, messenger pigeons, the ace of spades, until the very desire to take a stroll in strolls becomes more and more slender, the desire that transmutes into a stiletto, its slender blade in my heart. The somnambulists stretch out on beds of boards beneath which I am afraid to breathe, to scream, to fall asleep. I only make noises strictly necessary to my life, the imperceptible and disintegrative noise emitted by the images in my hair when the decomposition of things and beings above me begin to suffuse the exterior world with hallucinatory forms, immense sunflower-oil tractors disentangle from corpses, spill upon my forehead with a noise like urine, I am offered a bosom (I don't know why), a pear, an old frock coat in exchange for the description of a razor-sharpening machine, a feat that seems impossible to me because today I received a bouquet of artificial flowers without discovering who the author of this macabre farce, which, if she is a woman, I would surely forgive her, surely her lips conceal within their cherry flesh powdered with the dust of glacial kisses a slender, long needle, a drop of blood quivering on its point, a drop of blood in which I observe as in a magic mirror the random but sublime leisurely or convulsive appearance and disappearance of the flora, the trap on a field littered with trap-doors set by a woman with disheveled tresses who conceals beneath her left scapula a wide-blade scalpel scarred by an inscription, I follow with my head tumbling into a pitcher of water the heart of that drop of blood about which I could not say whether it is an eyeball or my lover's nipple presented on a teaspoon, my lover's nipple between my pallid lips, pallid like death, like ink, pallid like negation, my lips cut like a diamond in order for me to touch her dress and her death, the dress and death of my ventilated lover, ventilated as in the dream of a fan assembled from a thousand love letters, letters to kiss before committing suicide by all the love suicides, love suicides whose livid images may be perused as they glisten and gleam on my belly inside the umbilicus, where I preserve the pressed rose, the ribbons and the bows, the perfumes of the women over which we committed suicide so many times, so many times I waited for you by the side of the sidewalk, by the side of the ship, my shoes shining especially for you. How many times didn't I die? How many times nine times nine? And how many times is our tear more round than the universe? And the eyelashes?

THE DESIRED DESIRE

The alarm clock that space with its plaster hand confers upon this indistinct personage seated on a rock boasts two inebriated seals in place of its minute hand. Upon its dial, carved from blocks of ice, the insurgent and solemn numerals are inscribed with mirrors, the hour of the powder case mirror, the hour of the wardrobe mirror, the hour of the washstand mirror, the hour of the mirror chamber. I am agitated at the sight of a lone cow out upon a field, when a handsaw appearing out of nowhere severs her in two equal slices, like a baritone voice interrupted by a soprano. I am especially agitated by this arbitrary rapport which man, with angelic candor, with a sense of instant satisfaction developed to the point, have developed with, the two decrepit whores of human thought, space and time. These two vampires have sucked the human brain like a lemon. His stupidity, fear, and irremediable ugliness do not require supplementary explanations. It is enough to peruse this personage beneath a hat looking at his watch in order to understand cowardice, avarice and slavery; another personage sitting by the window of the railroad car is illustrative of oppression, conceit, and religious sentiment. I would like to become space and time myself in order to aim a powerful and definitive strike at the back of his head, his head the target of his slowly-ascending negation, like a grass of poisoned mirrors.

I knew a man who dreamed of far-away countries, for a night in a tavern or a temple, he would give his life, he would change his life. Another regrets his adolescence and scrutinizes the wrinkles on his forehead like so many horses that he wagered his life upon. Yet another, in his lamentable despair, in a sinister pursuit of immediate solutions brings about the birth of a child or purchases a place at the cemetery where he inscribes in marble letters: here lies. In each gesture, in each act, in each human enterprise I decipher these morbid and cynical words, his contact with the infinite exacted through his excrement, through acts of buying and selling (on the walls of a restaurant in Bucharest hangs a photograph, the size of one meter by sixty centimeters, underneath which is written Gheorghe Niculescu, 1889–1940, the founder of the magazine), this coprophiliac swallower of space and time divulges our comic position in the universe better than ten manuals of philosophy.

The distance between Gheorghe Niculescu, founder of the magazine, and Gheorghe Schopenhauer, founder of a philosophical system, proceeds from the comical to the sinister. Along this distance human thought lives out its innocent adventure from which solutions splinter like tombstones, macabre and delicious, a veritable anthology of black humor: the tailed piano of truth; the whale filled with burned stockings of space; two horse hooves shod with squishy horseshoes (the horseshoes could be manufactured from yogurt, egg whites, melted tallow or any other material of a consistency hesitating between solid and liquid) placed upon the shoulders of a woman (the woman is not clothed, she wears a ruby mask and long ruby stockings), each hoof promoting the injunction: to be; a gigantic drum abandoned for centuries on a calcareous expanse to stand in for Principles; six gala shays filled with their slit-throat drivers to stand in for Phenomenology; the idea of liberty, fraternity and equality manufactured from fish scales (carp scales for liberty and fraternity, pike scales for equality) affixed to a marble pedestal which may be moved from one place to another, to stand in for Reason; a few leaves of grass, a pigeon heart, the perfume of a mandragora and the cranium of a hyena prepared after any manual of magic and offered in dust form to a crow, to stand in for Certitude; the photo of a wealthy bride being wedded to a young worker and surrounded by family, friends, acquaintances and a few personalities such as Engels, Freud, Nietzsche, Beethoven, Columbus, Max Ernst, and Gherasim Luca, displayed in a photographer's shop window, to stand in for Concept; two eggs served in a cup to stand in for Reality; the popular image of Satan espied in hallucinatory fashion on the surface of a soup plate to stand in for the Particular and the General; a knife disappearing through a lady's décolletage, while in the next room a peace treaty is being signed, to stand in for Substance; an old surgeon to stand in for Abstract and Concrete; an operating table, operated by the old surgeon, absorbing the biological properties of the patients, to stand in for the Thing-in-Itself; the black hat-veil of that princess and her ring to stand in for Category; the scars of a palm tree painted by hand until you touch its fatigue, to stand in for Essence; an empty hole brought to the table as food, to stand in for Ethics; fists tightened on a doorknob enshrouding a few herbariums all at once although the fist holds butterflies and not a doorknob, one finger up the nose, to stand in for Metaphysics; for Self-Consciousness, a collection of postal stamps, next to which you keep with the same kind of care, like a shadow, the saliva you used to glue them; the Mediated and the Immediate, a hat or two; for Singular, for Absolute, for Logic, for Representation, for Limit, for Result, for Finality, for Duration, two chickens contemplating velvet or lightning, gliding along the lightning, a leisurely steel ball, what could contain a steel ball if not the roundness which surrounds it? if not the square that presup-

poses it? if not the eyelids, the kidney, the fear, the faraway?
How many times does it come to pass that each word I write
disgusts me, this writing that reduces the steel ball, the eye-
balls, the hand, the velvet and the faraway to the destiny of a
musical note and of a philosophical page, this writing by hand
and this lead hand so unreal, so inexistent, so false (or true,
it's all the same to me) in the window of the antique store, be-
ginning its existence (a finger up the nose for existence) only
at the instant when in my room it encounters the statue of the
medieval cavalier, which it besieges with an enigmatic finger,
between a few black steel balls brought by a woman who of-
fered me, in that language that only women and rocks can
speak, her round heart, her round ovaries, her round lips, her
round love (and when I say round it is a foregone conclusion
(1) that I am also saying square, as well as sweltering, as well
as I love you, as well as December) and when I say round I
would like (2) to say nothing, I am not interested (3) in saying
anything, I am not interested in communicating, or expressing
myself, what interests me is to provoke, to provoke the inside
of this world of borders in which I circulate between life and
death, between space and time, between love and hate, an en-
tire world of phenomena that escape me but that comprise
me, contain me like an aura containing the metallic head of
the somnambulist; the lead hand, this concrete expression,
naïve, ferocious expression of the amorous tryst, surrounded
by amorous ball bearings at the foot of an enamored cavalier,
between the legs of whom another hand, just as amoral, offers
a rose to the vista, what world of dreams, what world of awak-
ening does it unleash? what time, what space, what life, what
death are invented and automatically superimposed over our
lives and over our deaths? In this inhumane and anti-humane
world coming to life around me, almost without my will (all I
did was pronounce a formula, press a button, I am no more

than a snowball in the avalanche of determinants) you can't speak of desires seeking pleasures, this is something that is presupposed like something all too well known, like a necessary phase that has been long surpassed, what is of interest is only this petrified, chaotic pursuit of desires pursuing desires, pleasures being merely rapid stages, lightning-like and permanent, pleasures being what for a ball bearing would be its weight, an instantaneous pursuit from one desire to another desire, desire being through the nature of its message and diabolical consistency an inventor of other desires, kissing the mouth you invent the tongue, the tongue sends you to the clitoris, the clitoris suggests the knife with which you will unstring your victim, this victim, perennially dead, perennially alive like the simultaneous flux and reflux of love.

(1) a finger up the nose to stand in for "foregone conclusion."
(2) a finger up the nose for "I would like."
(3) a finger up the nose for "I am not interested."

THE KLEPTOBJECT SLEEPS

Round horses glide from one sidewalk to another, they are the memories of petrified cavaliers, their hands on a door. City mantled in gigantic oysters, traversed by trade winds, black city on the bottom of the planet, the bottom of the fountain, oozing out to the surface of the human epidermis like an emotional ulcer. Like an ulcer of sensation our fingertips quiver at every touch, ships with swollen sails crawl through them, vampiric apricots suck our fingerprints, mother-of-pearl fish are forced to face the wall as in a mass execution. What is going on here, there, inside, to the right, on the surface, on the head, on the water lily and velvet of our hearts? A thick, imperceptible mantle of crude oil rises slowly over the devastated ships that reroute it into the sewers, rises toward the skull, hair, and scrutinizes with foggy eyes each and every eclipse occurring in the outside world. Our heart, the only black sun that illumines us, our eyes, lips and fingers appear as if we gazed at, kissed and touched the things external to us through a foggy spyglass, a spyglass written with large letters directly upon the ink, a spectral spyglass. I spy a woman who is spying from her window in order to see me, who sees me. From both ends of the spyglass we spy on one another, we see and see each other with one single glance while with our free and flying hands we fling sharp-bladed stilettos at each other as if they were roses. Out of her eyes, the color of oceans, depart towards me two ships' cables from which a glove has been hung to dry. With a velocity reflecting the flux of oneiric notions, the woman takes the form of a curtain, a curtain from which two hearts pierced by an arrow bearing my initials fray away. Do I love myself? Do I suffer in my love for myself a narcissistic disappointment, the equivalent of my decision to shave alone at home with a straight razor a few centimeters below the epidermis, blood filling the washbowl, tears splashing upon my lips, lips on my lamentable, mutilated image? What follows is a sword, handed to me from the shadows by a personage perused from the back, a personage whose gender I cannot determine but whom I suspect is very beautiful. I kiss the sword while the personage disappears through a door and taste upon my lips the flavor of fresh ink. I scribble on the mirror with my lips "I adore you" and like a magic formula pronounced by mistake, the mirror image does not reproduce me, it is the personage from before, now perused from the front. It is indeed very beautiful, it is a woman, she can't be more than fourteen years old. What follows is a chamber that a man on a ladder paints yellow, the man wears a wig and I recognize him, it is Emmanuel Kant. At the foot of the ladder, stretched out on his belly, lies another Emmanuel Kant, leafing through a book containing the portrait of Emmanuel Kant. Contemplating his own portrait the man lying on the floor addresses the man on the ladder, speaking to him in jest: Quantity. The episode is very comical. It turns into a long string of zebras, interminable, followed by Breughel's blind men with the only difference that here, instead of falling, they throw themselves into the precipice, a very important difference because it de-Christianizes the painting and endows it with a unique flavor. The Breughel painting persists in the pursuant episode, this time the blind men, vested in soccer jerseys, pedal a bicycle-built-for-two while imparting well-meaning smiles to the public, like competitors in a bicycle race. It turns into a long black veil, fluttering over the people, above the people, while the citizens, yellow with fright, gaze with fixed eyeballs. This is followed by a young man exiting an automobile in front of a jewelry store in the city center, out of which he will exit in a few moments, a pearl necklace under his shirt next to his heart, next to the pistol. Or the gang of those with dyed hair, those three school-boys between twelve and sixteen who ran away from home last month and mingled among us in order to appropriate things valued at a few millions. Only an imbecilic, cretinized and cyn-ical justice could denounce their actions, more sublime than a crime, more innocent than incest. I was thinking of the sinis-ter Jean Valjean filching a loaf of bread leading to a lifetime behind bars, for whom justice proved itself to act with bound-less indulgence (the advantage being in fact that thousands of subsequent convictions that were concealed behind the lachry-mose Jean Valjean), I am thinking of the punishment I would apply to this obscurantist and moral shoplifter whom I would force to swallow the bread from below and excrete it from above, I would skin him alive like a putrid plum in order to make from his skin black gloves, black masks, black shoes with rubber soles and the entire inventory necessary for the ado-lescents of the gang of three with their dyed hair, dyed hair, this adorable travesty, this deceptive and prenatal travesty, this night fallen on their tresses, this translucent conspiracy, hallucinatory, ciphered, adorning the real with novel reality, with that transfiguration of simulacra, purloin a bicycle, a di-amond, a cascade, ten golden fountain pens, an aquarium, six adding machines, five hundred thousand lei from the bank, a top hat, a watermelon, a silvery fox, four automobile tires, a Longines wristwatch, a neck scarf, a tree, a river, an empty seltzer bottle, that is, precisely the items that belong to them, the gang of three with dyed hair appropriating these items, they are no longer any items, they distinguish themselves ex-actly as a leopard appears suddenly in our room and which looks nothing like those we envision somewhere in the jungle or circuses, the leopard of this object, the belladonna of this object, its electrifying agony, the platinum shiver that crosses us when we touch it, the sleep of this object, the subterranean gardens it encloses, the clang and clamor, its interior scratches and curtains suggest the lover's lips from which I steal a kiss, the kleptokiss, I steal in succession a bracelet, a photograph, a ribbon, an hour and I commit so many rapes, set so many fires, the kleptobracelet I put on in the evening in my room is more certain than a gender, the kleptophotograph more alive than the model, the ribbon is a new position for lovemaking while the kleptohour being, besides its relationship to time, what happens when that between people and things communicates a dimly oneiric atmosphere in which the symbol retains the consistency and consequences of the symbolized item, beneath a sky stabbed by lightning. This turns into a separation in a train station on the steps of a first-class car, the man's fingers being accidentally caught in the door and torn off, the man and the woman continue kissing, continue waving at each other with their handkerchief, their smiles simulating incognizance. It turns into a night in the open air on a blanket at the door of a forest. It turns into the alarm clock that we surreptitiously swallow like a pitcher of water trickling with a drop of iodine. It turns into rain. It turns into the leisurely undressing of a woman, an hour, two days. It turns into a net of wire pressing against the cheek of a child that another child is trying to kiss, the action taking place beneath a table at which adults are having their tea. It turns into the steppe. It turns into idiosyncrasy. It turns into the voices we hear behind a wall. Yesterday afternoon in a doctor's waiting room while waiting for the doctor to write me a prescription for an ointment against lice I surprised myself with my hand inside the coat-pocket of a stranger from which I stole a handkerchief. I offered this handkerchief/kleptohandkerchief exactly as it was, dirty and full of snot, to a woman who knew how to receive it tearfully, with appropriate gratitude like an homage, like a rose. She offered me her smile before I had a chance to steal it; in exchange I stole instead a hundred lei from her purse and the rouge on her lips. The systematic simulation of kleptomania stimulates a disproportionate frame of mind vis-à-vis the mediocrity of the object we appropriate; a misleading mediocrity, because during the process of theft, and even long after, the kleptobject eclipses all the useful objects, beautiful and expensive, lying about in its vicinity. In a world persisting in the sinister mythology of money, the kleptobject offers the possibility of negating it, replacing false external values with real, internal necessities. Certainly, the actual praxis of theft often takes on disgusting forms, money being the equivalent of a sum of rapid and superficial satisfactions, but theft followed by the burning of money, for instance, seems to me to replace any doubt relating to the concrete necessities that compel it. I am speaking of the kind of burning which is not caused by remorse, qualms of conscience or any other censorial values, I am speaking of a gratuitous burning, capricious and infantile. After plundering a bank, you buy a cookie, a tie, and bullets. You offer the money back to the first passerby or you burn it or spend it, these are details that do not change the inner principles you instated. I wouldn't be surprised if the day after a successful robbery I couldn't afford to eat, or if I squandered the money in bars in sorry fashion. Still, if I had twenty-five thousand lei, I would buy a very beautiful mirror I saw in the window of a furniture store. On the streets of this horrible city in which I am forced to expend my life these last years, I lug about a disgusting and devastated figure that the house windows reflect back to me as an insult. Separated from my friends who are scattered about the globe like an exigent leprosy, separated from them by multiple countries and an ocean serving as a conduit over which people make war with one another, I wake up alone each morning in my room and it is not by accident that my room's windows open directly out onto the military tribunal where each night I hear the sobs of the confined and convicted, alone in my room, always alone, even when my sex, in perpetual state of erection, magnetically lures from a distance a woman's skirt, even when the woman's skirt perpetually caresses me, indulgent, allowing, I still cannot hold back my agonized howl and even this howl that I emit furiously, desperately, whose resonance I feel must reach all the way to the farthest distances, all the way to humans, seals me ever more hermetically in my room, in my forest, where only the echo announces morning for me because the howl in the middle of the night collided with the mountaintop in the distance, rent a slice of rock and a ton of snow only to return between my teeth, my futile ferocious teeth, touchingly savage. In the state of stalking in which I find myself, seismograph of catastrophe, inflamed and infuriated, an epileptic quaver in the corner of my lips, alert and active, perpetually alert and active, I await for a few years now a letter, a pack of dynamite, a monstrous woman, a poem written in an unknown tongue, an erotic position in which the partners electrocute each other, a prophetic dream, a sudden jolt of sensual derangement, a spontaneous disclosure of a crucial magic formula, I await with fists clawing my nerves, eyes steadfastly rooted upon a diamond, lips still humid from kisses planting themselves randomly on treebark, foreheads, rocks. Surely the instant I write these lines a terrifying infernal machine of desire is powered up, it may be me who powers it up, maybe faraway friends or those I don't know yet, but the precarious condition of life we are forced to live under causes our most incandescent flight to resemble a forced landing and agony.

I write these lines in the hope that they will be read by a king of thieves ferocious enough to receive me among his peers, a band of civic thieves, civic assassins, civic brigands with whom I would like to spend the rest of the days remaining till the end of the war.

October 24, 1942

ONTOPOETICS,
OR THE TRANS-SURREALIST PATH

by Petre Răileanu

Gherasim Luca
Bucharest, 1913–Paris, 1994

The arrival in this world of Gherasim Luca, "a name and a wandering," was one of those miraculous encounters that, along the path of his entire life, he never ceased provoking and "objectifying," both in life and poetry. Two realities blindly wander in distant orbits and, although no apparent or inherent necessity destines them to meet, they come into contact, intersect, and give birth to a new planet. The desire of the adolescent Salman Locker, who was preparing to make his debut in poetry and looking for a new place to emerge in life other than the accident of birth, encountered the news of the death of "Gherasim Luca, Archimandrite of Mount Athos and illustrious linguist." Just as initiation rites imitate the wisdom of nature, death generates life. For the young Romanian *etranjuif*— stranjew, as he would moniker himself—with his unique sense of assigning precision to ambiguity, this name was the first "found object" and the first sign of the coherence that establishes itself between living, dying, and writing.

Gherasim Luca is a phantom, at best a fiction distilled from his work. Early on, his texts were placed under the sign of a programmatic imperative: the reinvention of another universe unbound by the myth of Oedipus. To reinvent life, love, and death is what any poet worthy of the name does naturally, but Luca conferred to it the anti-Oedipal fingerprint that marked his existence and work. A parallel revolution took place on the level of language, perceptible especially in his French work. Luca placed us in the presence of revelation when he led us to discover that the "sacred" associates with "massacre," that life *(la vie)* is present in the void *(le vide)*, and that love *(l'amour)* is inseparable from death *(la mort)*. These examples do not simply emerge from phonetic chance encounters but nourish substance in the implacable logic of the poetic word.

His first texts published in Bucharest, especially in the magazine *Alge*, in the avant-garde ambiance of the 1930s, reveal a surprising familiarity with modern poetics. As with his immediate predecessors, Tristan Tzara, Ion Vinea, Ilarie Voronca, Stephan Roll, and Geo Bogza, whose work he had read in the avant-garde publications, the deconstruction of syntax and the renewal of poetic language occupy an important place, as does the new type of definitive image as the place of encounter for distant realities. A few remnants of grandiose rhetoric or, at times, repetitions, symmetrical alliances, proper names with exotic resonances, constitute the last vestiges of the great symbolist era. But starting with these texts, Luca committed himself to the path of the direct discourse, like the "punch of a fist," long theorized by his predecessors but practiced only very timidly. Luca's wager was not to transform each trope and metaphor into the absurd, as Paul Celan would later attempt, but purely and simply to renounce them. The poems put into play a series of extremely violent images, but it must be noted that for Gherasim Luca violence was the fruit of a cold delirium; lucidity was always active, lending its surprisingly meticulous expression to the formidable sensorial disorder in his poetry. Crime, suicide, self-destruction, and self-mutilation are often present in these texts. The contemplation of his own fragmented being, as in a dream or as if referring to another or a double, anticipated the experiences later described in *The Dead Death* or, on a visual plane, the cubomanias that revealed their constitutive sadomasochism.

Social revolt cannot be separated from the other themes present in the texts of those years; it impregnates the new poetic program, *Poetry we wish to make.* This collective manifesto marks a rupture vis-à-vis the avant-garde movement that preceded him and which is accused of reducing poetry to a mere technical issue. Breton (convulsive beauty), Lautréamont (poetry will be made by all) are allusively present in this text, but the manifesto eschews the cultural or artistic aspect in favor of "an elementary aesthetics of life." A decisive step in the direction of surrealism was taken; the others would follow: a two-year sojourn to Paris from 1938 to 1940, at the same time as the poet Gellu Naum, the meeting with André Breton and his entourage, but especially the reencounter with Victor Brauner, the great initiator of all forms of thought and expression likely to precipitate the revelation of the supersensible world. Outside of a few misunderstandings or quarrels, Luca and Brauner remained indestructibly connected through a kind of fraternity of disquiet and through the dangers assumed by the hypostasis of explorations of the interior depths, an equivalent of what they called "life in life."

At the beginning of 1941, the Romanian surrealist group was formed and its program may be synthesized in the following terms: rehabilitation of the dream, conferring upon it the status of objective reality; elimination of its latent content (which is nothing but simplified summary of the Oedipal complex) in favor of its manifest content; to accord all attention to desire, considered as a kind of code of human personality.

Romanian surrealism was essentially experimental, and its lived reality represented its most pregnant particularity that distinguished it in context of international surrealism.

The Passive Vampire, written in 1941 and published at the end of the war in 1945, was Luca's first properly surrealist text. It is a distillation of the poet's theoretical options, as well as his position within the context of surrealism. Poetry, dream, magic enter the universe of metamorphosis and transmutations where time is no longer linear, it dilates, allowing displacement without impediments, backwards and forwards as in space, a world in which the Possible replaces the Real. Like the passive vampire, Luca owns the literal and symbolic instrument and the fulcrum of support that allows his suspension between one world and the other, an escape from the universe under the reign of the Oedipal myth and situated beneath the sign of the General Absolute Paralytic, which is death in the realm of our interior delirium. This instrument is the ineffable fulcrum of dialectics and the starting point is the subconscious, thrusting perpetually forward in the domain of unguided thought. With these trump cards in hand, renouncing any path of return, Luca dedicated himself with passion to a delirious, demiurgic approach. *The Inventor of Love,* followed by *I Roam the Impossible,* represented a new step: the explicit construction of the non-Oedipal universe. "Everything must be reinvented, no-thing exists anymore in the whole world," resonates as a leitmotif throughout the text. Birth, like love and death, must be reinvented; it holds captive the "axiomatic humanoid of Oedipus," scattered like an "obscurantist epidemic" for the last few thousand years. To refuse birth, to abjure any axiom, "even if it boasts of the appearance of a certitude," this is the proposed solution that would prepare the arrival of the man without a past, without reference points, without preconception. Love must also be reinvented, especially love, and the poet assumes the freedom of not loving a being conceived by the Creator. The beloved woman is "unborn," her appearance in the world is similar to the appearance of a new planet. She is not a complete being, she must be invented and reinvented each moment, she is synthesis, the meeting place of the bodies of many women, of fragments, of diamonds, of mouths, of eyelashes, eyelids, hair, veils. The woman is a creation of the artist, like the cubomanias, the result of the intentional confusion between the Possible and the Real. With characteristic facility, Luca comprised within the same segment of text many registers, while infusing the same episode, whose appearance is that of a poetic theorem, with the very darkly malefic passion of a sacrilege-crime and the solemnity of a cosmogony.

The Praying Mantis Appraised was written in Romanian in 1942 and edited in 1945. After more than forty years, the French edition retains its prose form, thus preserving the poem's aspect of fluid magma despite its misleading organization in multiple units. It contains all of the themes and obsessions present in his previous work, less the programmatic-theoretical fury of *The Inventor of Love* or *The Passive Vampire*, and constitutes the hallucinatory *mise-en-scene* of the savage dream that tames the dreamer. Despite the "poetized Satanism" present in each sentence, the text heralds the presentiment of a luminous renewal, supporting itself upon the oneiric mechanism playing the role of fulcrum acting on the world, like the successive metamorphosis from *The Foreshadowed Castle*. This dialectic appears in *The Desired Desire* and offers the image of a volute that connects the uncreated to its foreseeable finality. The word has not crossed the teeth's threshold, as Homer said, but contains, both symbolically and literally, the actuality it expresses and will transfer into the sphere of reality. The desired desire is that place where "time and

space disappear, where death is animated and life is alive..."
The desired desire is the serpent that bites its own tail,
Ouroboros, the alchemists' emblem and reference to Nicolas
Flamel, to whom this syntagma belongs, *le désir désire,* which
demonstrates the simultaneous character of Luca's double
strategy: the quest for poetry and regal art, and also the pro-
portion with which he aims to endow his quest (the contact
with the point of convergence of contraries, the penetration
of regions where harmony outside time and space reigns, and
from which life extracts its sap).

In fact, the direct mention of Nicolas Flamel and his mys-
terious journey to Spain (which yielded a single accomplish-
ment: "to forget a dream") as well as the appropriation of his
syntagma *(The Desired Desire)* recalls the path of initiations,
of all those who seek the "gold of time." The experiments un-
dertaken in the world of objects and the revelation of their
mediumistic qualities in *The Passive Vampire* or in a lost text,
To Onericize the World, as in the woman-medium, as she ap-
pears in *I Roam The Impossible,* which Luca, mysteriously, left
in the original Romanian, were his own contributions to this
path that leads to the heart of the miraculous *(le merveilleux).*
As the Romanian surrealists informed Breton in a letter at the
beginning of the 1950s, spiritism and operational magic con-
stituted the object of their interest. From a radically modified
perspective difficult to understand today, they cited homeop-
athy as a subversive domain:

> As a result of particular circumstances, the
> group familiarized itself in part with judici-
> ary astrology, tarot, and the so-called primi-
> tive arts, but also became interested in
> "spiritism," homeopathy, operational magic,
> depending on the circumstances.

Even more revealing is the tendency of the Bucharest group of "organizing in a secret center, in the initiatory fashion." *The Praying Mantis Appraised,* like other texts of the Romanian surrealists, confer a narrative form to certain stages that lead to the philosopher's stone.

The surrealist painters took their experience to the point that allowed them to contemplate the invisible and transpose it into the visible. The final stage of poetic expression is silence. Paul Celan aimed at the involution of language, of the poetic word toward a last syllable, stranger to the word, while his poems are garnered like indestructible stalactites of silence. Luca provided another name to replace the word poetry that seemed denatured to him: *ontophony,* or *silenceophone.*

The reader of this reputedly untranslatable author will be quickly trained in the luminous subterranean passages of his work, captured in the traps that the text multiplies at every step. Luca's work functions like a palimpsest, in which multiple strata of significance and stylistic registers coexist in an ambiguous simultaneity. The act of translation, however difficult, situates itself in the regions of exaltation, because revelations are multi-lingual. Just like silence, just like forgetfulness. This translation into English, effectuated with virtuosity by Julian and Laura Semilian, is a witness to this reality, an attempt to bring to light the coherence of the poetic text, the complete and stormy equivalence between the signifier and the signified, between part and whole, between sky and earth. Like Tabula Smaragdina! Intensifying the light of day or "darkening the dark."

Paris

TRANSLATOR BIOS

Born in Romania, Julian Semilian is a poet, translator, novelist, and filmmaker. After a twenty-four-year career as a film editor in Hollywood where he has worked on more than fifty movies and TV shows, Semilian presently teaches film editing at the University of North Carolina School of the Arts. Among his published works are *Osiris with a Trombone Across the Seam of Insubstance* (novel), *A Spy in Amnesia* (novel), and *Transgenger Organ Grinder* (poems), all from Spuyten Duyvil Press. As a translator, Julian has concentrated on the Jewish Romanian avant-garde of the twenties, thirties, and forties, and has published *The Romanian Poems of Paul Celan* (Green Integer) and *Nostalgia* by Mircea Cartarescu (New Directions). As a filmmaker, he has recently finished *Devotees of the Precipitate,* a film detailing the shadow of Man Ray.

Laura Semilian enjoys researching and writing, particularly about history. She regularly collaborates with her husband in rendering Romanian poetry and literature into her native English. A soprano, she has composed scores for his films, and has performed as a soloist with symphony orchestras and opera companies throughout the U.S.

TITLES FROM BLACK WIDOW PRESS

TRANSLATION SERIES

Approximate Man and Other Writings
by Tristan Tzara. Translated and edited
by Mary Ann Caws.

Art Poétique by Guillevic. Translated
by Maureen Smith.

Capital of Pain by Paul Eluard.
Translated by Mary Ann Caws,
Patricia Terry, and Nancy Kline.

Chanson Dada: Selected Poems
by Tristan Tzara. Translated with an
introduction and essay by Lee Harwood.

*Essential Poems and Writings of
Robert Desnos: A Bilingual Anthology*
Edited with an introduction and essay
by Mary Ann Caws.

*Essential Poems and Writings of
Joyce Mansour: A Bilingual Anthology*
Translated with an introduction by
Serge Gavronsky.

EyeSeas (Les Ziaux)
by Raymond Queneau. Translated with
an introduction by Daniela Hurezanu
and Stephen Kessler.

The Inventor of Love & Other Writings
by Gherasim Luca. Translated by Julian
and Laura Semilian. Introduction by
Andrei Codrescu. Essay by Petre
Răileanu.

Last Love Poems of Paul Eluard
Translated with an introduction by
Marilyn Kallet.

Love, Poetry (L'amour la poésie)
by Paul Eluard. Translated with an essay
by Stuart Kendall.

*Poems of André Breton:
A Bilingual Anthology*
Translated with essays by Jean-Pierre
Cauvin and Mary Ann Caws.

Poems of A.O. Barnabooth
by Valery Larbaud. Translated by
Ron Padgett and Bill Zavatsky.

The Sea and Other Poems by Guillevic.
Translated by Patricia Terry. Introduc-
tion by Monique Chefdor.

To Speak, to Tell You? by Sabine Sicaud
Translated by Norman R. Shapiro. Intro-
duction and notes by Odile Ayral-Clause.

forthcoming translations

*Essential Poems and Writings
of Jules Laforgue*
Translated and edited by Patricia Terry.

*Essential Poems and Writings
of Pierre Reverdy*
Translated by Mary Ann Caws and
Patricia Terry.

Furor and Mystery & Other Writings
by René Char. Edited and translated by
Mary Ann Caws and Nancy Kline.

I Want No Part in It and Other Writings
by Benjamin Péret. Translated with an
introduction by James Brook.

La Fontaine's Bawdy
by Jean de la Fontaine. Translated with
an introduction by Norman R. Shapiro.

Preversities: A Jacques Prévert Sampler
Translated and edited by
Norman R. Shapiro.

The Big Game by Benjamin Péret.
Translated with an introduction by
Marilyn Kallet.

MODERN POETRY SERIES

An Alchemist with One Eye on Fire
by Clayton Eshleman

Archaic Design by Clayton Eshleman

Backscatter: New and Selected Poems
by John Olson

The Caveat Onus
by Dave Brinks
The complete cycle, four vols. in one.

Crusader-Woman
by Ruxandra Cesereanu. Translated
by Adam J. Sorkin. Introduction by
Andrei Codrescu.

Forgiven Submarine
by Ruxandra Cesereanu and
Andrei Codrescu

The Grindstone of Rapport:
A Clayton Eshleman Reader
Forty years of poetry, prose, and
translations by Clayton Eshleman.

Packing Light:
New and Selected Poems
by Marilyn Kallet

Signal from Draco:
New and Selected Poems
by Mebane Robertson

forthcoming modern poetry titles

Anticline by Clayton Eshleman

Concealments and Caprichos
by Jerome Rothenberg

Curdled Skulls: Poems of Bernard Bador
Translated by Clayton Eshleman and
Bernard Bador

Fire Exit by Robert Kelly

Larynx Galaxy by John Olson

Selected Poems of Amina Said
Translated by Marilyn Hacker

LITERARY THEORY/BIOGRAPHY SERIES

Revolution of the Mind:
The Life of André Breton
by Mark Polizzotti
Revised and augmented edition.

WWW.BLACKWIDOWPRESS.COM